WHAT PEOPLE ARE SAYING ABOUT

MERLIN: ONCE AND FUTURE WIZARD

I've always loved reading tales of Merlin. In this book Elen
Sentier gives a fascinating and personal account of the magical
lessons she has learnt through shamanic journeying with the
most famous wizard of the British Isles.
Lucya Starza, author of *Pagan Portals – Candle Magic*

Merlin – Once and Future Wizard is a grand and imaginative work
that introduces the reader to the many faces of the mysterious
Merlin. Combining history and myth, personal experiences and
teaching stories into a vibrant whole that captivates readers, this
little book will invite you to seek out Merlin in the living world
of today as well as the tales of old. Truly a delightful read.
Morgan Daimler, author of *Fairycraft, Pagan Portals – The
Morrigan* and *Pagan Portals – Brighid*

T0154599

Pagan Portals
Merlin:

Once and Future Wizard

Pagan Portals
Merlin:

Once and Future Wizard

Elen Sentier

Winchester, UK
Washington, USA

First published by Moon Books, 2016
Moon Books is an imprint of John Hunt Publishing Ltd., Laurel House, Station Approach,
Alresford, Hants, SO24 9JH, UK
office1@jhpbooks.net
www.johnhuntpublishing.com
www.moon-books.net

For distributor details and how to order please visit the 'Ordering' section on our website.

Text copyright: Elen Sentier 2016

ISBN: 978 1 78535 453 3
978 1 78535 454 0 (ebook)
Library of Congress Control Number: 2016949318

A CIP catalogue record for this book is available from the British Library.

Design: Stuart Davies

Printed and bound by CPI Group (UK) Ltd, Croydon, CR0 4YY, UK

We operate a distinctive and ethical publishing philosophy in all
areas of our business, from our global network of authors to
production and worldwide distribution.

CONTENTS

'There is no consciousness without pain. People will do anything, no matter how absurd, in order to avoid facing their own soul. One does not become enlightened by imagining figures of light, but by making the darkness conscious.'

C. G. Jung

1

Who is Merlin?

This book is about the intimate lifelong relationship I've had with Merlin and what I've learned from him. I learned to know him as a little child and that knowing, we call it kenning in the old ways, has grown all my life. I now live in one of his places, a place where one of his stories has taken root, in the Welsh Marches on the borders of Wales and England. I see him here in many of his guises ... he's huge, ancient, wise and powerful, and also kindly, but he's a trickster, as all the best teachers are, so you do have to be on top of your game with him.

The book's title – *The Once and Future Wizard* – somewhat gives away who he is. The word *once* means before, past, as in 'once upon a time', and Merlin is from the past, the very ancient past. His essence goes back all the way in our human journey on Planet Earth and very likely he was around, as were the other powers we call gods, from the Earth's very beginning, maybe even before that. The word *future* means just that, the future, what is ahead of us, and Merlin is our future too, he holds the threads of all possible futures in his hands. The future means at least all the next several billion years, however-long, until the sun becomes a red giant and burns us all back to our component atoms again. Merlin will likely go on even beyond that, for the death of our sun is an end that enables another beginning. The atoms that come apart then will come together again somewhere else, into new forms of life, and so the cycle continues.

And at the centre, between past and future, stands Merlin.

Merlin is a liminal being. Liminal means a threshold, a place between past and future, between here and there, between one world and another ... and he is always standing at that threshold. He *is* that place. And that ever-changing but constant threshold is

now, the here-and-now, and it's constantly in motion like the sea, never the same from one instant of time to the next.

The **now** is the only place that is real. Past and future are memories and dreams, they are not where we are, and those memories and dreams are like virtual reality games, great fun but not genuine or authentic to the life we're currently living. Now is the only place we are able to live, but most of us are rarely conscious there. So many of us live in the next moment, or the previous moment, remembering or dreaming, so we never really know the present. We're getting ready to go out for a lovely evening with friends and our mind is not on the getting ready but imagining how it will be when we get there, how our friends will like our new dress, the compliments we'll get on the new tie. Driving home after the evening, our mind is not fully on the drive but on remembering what went well and the lumpy bits that didn't go so good. We do not live in the here-and-now.

Merlin is about living in the here-and-now. He *is* that continuous and ever-changing threshold that is reality.

As the poet TS Eliot says in Quartet No 1: Burnt Norton, *'humankind cannot bear very much reality'*. We're worse than cats at change and that's unfortunate as it's truly the only place we can live. We like to live in what we know, have known, how it always has been – which, of course, it hasn't. We want things to get back to normal. We are afraid of change. Standing at, let alone crossing, thresholds and so leaving the old behind to go to the new, going from the known to the unknown, is very difficult for us. But, unconsciously, we do it all the time. The trick is learning to be continuously and consciously aware that you stand in the middle of change all the time, whatever is going on. Trust me, or rather trust Merlin, it really does work!

Merlin is there for all of us. This incarnation, this time around, I've known him consciously for all my life, since I was a baby, and he's here all the time for me. I walk between worlds as we call it in the old ways of Britain, a phrase from one of our old awenyddion, seannachie as they call them in Scottish Gaelic. His name was Thomas of Erceldoune, but you may know him better as Thomas the Rhymer from the old song and his story is well worth reading although you will have to go to several sources to piece it together, there's my own version on my website.

Walking between worlds means having a foot in the everyday world *at the same time* as having the other foot in otherworld; I am here-and-there at the same time. No, I'm not nuts, if you saw me in the pub you'd just think I was an ordinary elderly woman – for I am! But I'm also an awenydd – it means spirit-keeper in the old Brythonic tongue – I live with otherworld *as well as* with thisworld, and Merlin taught me how to do this.

What I've learned is available to any and all of us, he will come to anyone who calls out to him that they want to learn, are ready to learn. But you have to mean it!

This work isn't a cute little weekend course that you can put away in its box on Sunday night and come back to 'normality'. It's your life, a lifetime commitment. That doesn't mean you have to become an ascetic, give up everyday life and your mobile phone, live a spartan and abstemious existence – no, far from it. Merlin needs those he works with to be deeply involved in everyday human life as well as learning as much as they can about the unseen worlds. He wants us to mingle and twine and integrate spirit and matter, not to dash unthinkingly and hedonistically between the weekend trip and the working week. To do that, to live *either* in the everyday *or* in spirit, is as much use to him as an ashtray on a motorbike!

Knowing Merlin

So how do we come to know Merlin for who he truly is?

To know him we have to put aside all the scripts we most of us have learned and grown up with, lived with all our lives; all those scripts we got from our parents and at school, from our friends, and from employers, bank managers, tax men and politicians. He really and truly isn't in them. They're about conformity, about making life comfortable amongst millions, billions, of other people, and Merlin most certainly is not about comfort. He's about stretching and growing, expanding the envelope, going beyond our limits, crossing frontiers, letting go and jumping off cliffs. He's about joy.

As I said before, letting go of what we know is hard for humans, we want things to be normal and we all resist like mad if somebody tells us things really are not as we believe them to be, and want them to be. But when, with Merlin's help, we start to get the hang of change and begin to walk the old ways, we climb out of this pattern of conformity. I come from a background with a lot less cultural conformity-baggage to drop, so letting go has always been less of a problem for me. I'm part of a group – larger than you might think – of folk who have been in the old ways from birth, and their families before them. For me and mine Merlin is a reality, he's really there and no question about it, and that makes a huge difference to how you feel about change.

Most people come through birth with a serious dose of spiritual amnesia, they remember little or nothing of the other-world they've just left. Many children do go through the stage of what psychology and parenting books call 'imaginary friends', but this often results in parents and school quashing such ideas with the intention of making the kids normal. So the children do as they're told in order to gain the love and attention they need, and this need for approval continues on through life until and unless some form of awakening happens and is able to birth itself without further inhibition from society. With all this peer-pressure on people to conform, being able to let go and make room in your thinking so you really can get to know Merlin is not an easy job.

Awakenings do happen, and in all sorts of ways. When they do it's good to find someone you can talk about all this with, someone who's been there, done that, got the T-shirt and licked the stamp, someone who isn't going to be afraid of what you say or try to tell you to get a grip and be normal. It's even better if you can find someone who knows Merlin intimately and is willing to walk beside you on your own journey to know him – and there are quite a few of us about if you go look. Doing it completely on your own, with nobody to talk to, is incredibly hard and many would say impossible. The experiences are just so wonderful, and they can be so far from what is normally acceptable and, indeed, off-the-wall to many, that someone who's gone there before you is a real help. You don't feel alone, and they help you stop that nasty subliminal feeling that you really are nuts.

Meeting Merlin

Having, building, making a relationship with Merlin is so worthwhile.

I'm by no means the only person I know who has a deep and strong relationship with Merlin, many of my friends and students do too. It's most certainly not the sort of relationship to ever get jealous about!

Perhaps you already have an idea of how huge he is – like he tries to show us when he shapeshifts into the figure of Custennin, Lord of the Animals. Such a being, power, mover and shaper, will need far more than just little me to help him get the work done that he needs done, so he comes to a great many of us. Each of us has different skills and abilities. I know artists, craftspeople, singers and musicians, writers, herbalists, woodsmen (like my Uncle Jack), people who work with animals and birds, fishermen, architects and builders, policemen, hunters, trackers and stalkers, and wildlife photographers who work with him. Even some of my old friends from when I worked for the MoD, folk in the Army, Air Force, Royal Marines and the SAS/SBS, know and work with him. Oh yes, Merlin gets about and not just amongst the luv-n-lite brigade either.

He's been a part of my life for all of my life, has helped me, guided and guarded me when I needed it, and kicked my butt when I need it too! But I share him with everyone else, we're all part of his team, his gang as many of us call it, and the longer I work with him the more of the gang I get to know. That's seriously reassuring; I too like to know I'm not on my own, that not only are there many otherworldly friends but there are many in thisworld too.

Having a relationship with Merlin does require you to be conscious, awake and aware, and to have a strong personality as well as an excellent sense of humour. You really need the latter because he will send you down the shop for a tin of striped paint on those days when you're being particularly dumb and naïve! But that's the case with all otherworld teachers, you have to be prepared to trip over your feet and fall flat on your arse then get up saying ouch, and maybe swearing, but definitely laughing at your own daftness. You have to know when you screwed up and be happy to admit it.

First Meeting

I still remember lying in bed, in my high-sided cot up in the attic bedroom. I must have been about one-and-a-half or maybe two. Looking on Google Earth it seems Number 9 East Street, Okehampton, is now a purple Co-op Funeralcare palace, but back then it was where we lived. It was my aunts' house, a big three-storey terrace building where my aunts also had their hairdressing business. Under the arch, which is now a car park, was Gunn's pop factory.

Dad had come to tell me the bedtime story as he did every evening. I loved the stories, and this evening he began to tell me the story of a man who lived in the woods, under an apple tree, with a young pig. As always, Dad stopped the story halfway through so we'd continue it the next night. He'd been watching my eyelids droop so he knew when to stop, kissed me goodnight and went out, softly closing the door behind him.

I always had a night-light candle as a baby. I don't recall being afraid of the dark but I do remember loving the shadows flickering up the walls from the candle. Now, as I lay watching them make patterns, I saw a figure begin to materialise at the end of the cot. It was a tall, slim man with a long thin face, his dark hair hung over the collar of the tunic he wore under a leather waistcoat. He looked a bit like my Uncle Jack but I knew it wasn't him. His dark eyes held me, there was a light flickering in them and the lids crinkled as his long, thin mouth smiled at me. 'Hello,' he said.

I whispered hello back and lay there holding my breath. Who was this? He felt good and I wanted him to stay. He came round to the side of the cot and touched my hand. The skin tingled like electricity.

'Hello, little one,' he said. 'You're a friend of mine and we're going to know each other very well. I'll come to see you every day but now it's time for you to go to sleep, to dream … and dream of me.' His fingers touched my eyelids.

I certainly remember the dreams. They've continued all my life and I now know they were my first experience of travelling, journeying, for our folk have always worked and travelled through dreams.

Looking back now with my mind's eye I can still see that room, the flickering candlelight and the tall figure at the end of my cot. It's something I'll never forget and I hope that when I die he will be there to lead me back over the threshold into otherworld.

That figure from my babyhood experience was Merlin. I didn't learn this for a while. Dad told me lots of stories about him, but it was a couple of years before I cottoned on that the figure who visited me was the same person as the one in Dad's stories. When I did know who he was I told Dad. He just nodded and smiled.

Dad's stories told me lots about Merlin and Merlin would show the stories to me again as moving pictures in my mind's eye, like a film of the bedtime stories inside my head. I know now these films were another version of travelling, journeying.

Merlin is a legendary figure and best known in the everyday world as the wizard from the Arthurian stories. He's been written and rewritten, bent and twisted and reshaped by every generation since at least 400AD/500AD, some 1,600 years and maybe even longer. Television still creates new versions of Merlin and his stories. Of the more recent versions I find I like Mary Stewart's trilogy the best, her style and writing come closest to my own experience of him.

But it's a whole different experience when you actually meet him. He, like all the Powers, is a shapeshifter and so able to appear to each of us in the way that we will find most appealing. The TV versions that I don't like certainly do appeal to others and so enable him to be known by more people. This has happened all through his written history as each generation builds and discovers the Merlin most acceptable to them. Continuously changing and shifting.

2

Merlin in History, Stories and Poetry

Merlin is our wizard here in Britain. He is a spirit of the land and Britain is called Clas Merlin in some of the stories, meaning Merlin's place.

One thing to remember right from the start is that Merlin is far, far older than the Arthurian legends or indeed any of the written history about him. Our written records only go back about 2,000 years, which is no time at all, even in human history. Interestingly, a BBC article of 20th Jan 2016 tells of recent research that shows our fairy stories are very much older than historians previously thought. Using techniques normally employed by biologists, Durham University anthropologist, Dr Jamie Tehrani, studied links between stories from around the world and found some tales that were far, far older than the earliest literary records. In fact, Dr Tehrani traced several stories back more than 5,000 years ago to when Eastern and Western Indo-European languages split. The stories' roots are prehistoric, dating back to the Bronze Age. It's quite possible (likely even) that all our stories are this old, if we come to be convinced of this it's another area of change we're going to need Merlin's help with as it will set our current ideas of 'progress' right on their heads. And we'll need his help getting to their roots so we can understand what they really say rather than translating them into modern-speak with modern concepts that are not what the stories are about at all.

Nowadays, there's an absolute plethora of books, writing, films, stories, pictures and legends about Merlin; some good, some not so good and some just downright awful, at least in my opinion. It all depends on what you're looking at and where you're looking from and, of course, what you want to either do with, or gain from, your story or history.

Merlin's tales tell us he has had many incarnations, in many places around the country and indeed around Europe, add in that many of them have apparently been at the same time, so you cannot think of them in linear time, and you see why he confuses academics like crazy! If we really want to get to know him then Merlin requires us to think outside the box. We will lose the plot entirely if we get stuck in university libraries or lectures, or between the hide-bound covers of some ancient tome. Most of all he needs us *not to want* to have a perfect answer about who he is – and that not-wanting is hard to do. He is never still, he never stops moving, never stops growing and changing and evolving, he is continually in motion in both time and space, and he is always with us, just as he promises in the stories.

To know Merlin is much easier once we're able to see him and this means seeing him in everything around us, in all of nature, for this is what he is. As Breton writer Jean Markale says, Merlin is a spirit of nature, perhaps *the* spirit of nature or rather the spirit in its masculine form. He appears in many guises, as the Green Man, the wildman of the forest, as an old wizard, a young boy, or a giant herdsman with a huge club, or a stag. He can and does appear as anything we need in order that he may become visible to us.

I said the masculine form of the spirit, for Merlin partners with the feminine. His partner is called Vivien or Nimue (and other names too) and she is also known for a deer-woman, especially among the Breton people. And she, too, is a doorkeeper, a threshold-keeper. We'll go into his relationship with her later, it's much deeper than the Victorian romantic *femme fatale* she is normally portrayed as.

As you've probably gathered, this book is not yet another academic study of the various writings about Merlin. I've read a lot about him, and my Dad told me stories about him since I was a baby, but my greatest experience and knowing of him has been through the personal encounters that have happened all my life.

Having a personal relationship with him makes possible so much knowing, understanding and hopefully wisdom. He wants as many folk as possible to get to know him, for only so can he help us change to become again able to *live-with* our land and with the whole Earth.

Merlin has become legendary ... but what does that mean? In academic terms the word legendary is often thought only to mean imaginary, made up and therefore untrue, but if you go and look the word up you find it means *renowned, remarkable* and *extraordinary*, and that is just how the real Merlin is.

The word legendary is also said to mean fairy-tale, fabled and fabulous, and both Merlin and his stories are certainly all of this. In Britain, tales and stories have always been our way of telling the lore on to our children and back to ourselves as well, we are known for taleweavers. We all love stories whether we read them, listen to them, watch them in a film or a play, run them through our mind's eye, or play them on Xbox. Stories enchant us, and to en-chant something means to sing it into life, in this case Merlin's stories sing us into life as my Dad's stories about him did for me. The whole concept of legend and enchantment needs rethinking to become broader and deeper, and so better able to include more reality.

And what are fairy stories? Who are the Faer? Are they part of Merlin's people? Is he part of the Faer? The Faer are the fairy folk, the bright ones, the little people, the sidhe, and all their ilk. Faer is a word and name common in many forms throughout European folklore. In the parlance of the modern shamanic practitioner they are part of 'non-ordinary reality' – I find that term, *non-ordinary*, both longwinded and difficult to swallow.

My background is not that of core shamanism or the modern shamanic practitioner, but of someone who grew up in the ancient tradition that has been in hiding for 2,000 years. The modern core shaman stuff has some similarities to our old ways, but also many differences, and this intimate knowing – that we call kenning – of Spirit itself and of spirits, including great spirits like Merlin – is not usually found in the modern core practice. But I grew up to ken, to know, all of otherworld as well as I knew my own family. My family, the old ones of the villages where I grew up, and many of the people I know now including my friends, all *know* and *ken* the Faer and we include them in our everyday reality. It's those who don't have this kenning that are to us 'non-ordinary'. We all get up close and personal with Spirit, including Merlin, for this is what he wants. Merlin is indeed part of the company of the Faer.

Most people today have little or no idea of our old traditions so when they want a spiritual practice they go abroad, overseas, out of our land, for it. The current fashion is for South American and Mexican traditions, which include plant medicine and drugs. People just don't know where to look for it here in Britain and they've been told, until they believe it, that our old customs are just a load of primitive superstitions or else have been made up in modern times and are not really native or indigenous.

We old ones have been hiding here in plain sight for the past 2,000 years and, in consequence, we're very good at it. That's why most people don't know we exist. Merlin has been conflated with all of this superstition so he has become related more to Harry Potter in most people's minds than to the enormous and powerful spirit of the land that he is. Remember, one of the names of Britain is Clas Merlin ... Merlin's Land. Merlin is the spirit and essence, the creative life-force and kernel of our land. He has been incarnate in many times and many places throughout Britain, and so has given physical personification and embod-iment to a very deep principle. He is the epitome and archetype of the *walker between worlds* ... what we know nowadays as the shaman.

As we learn more about him we find he goes back into a deep past of which we have no modern-style records. The only way to explore that past is in ways not many archaeologists or academics can tolerate, although some have, and that's journeying. If you're willing to open up to the possibilities of journeying then you'll gradually discover more and more of him.

The Written Word

There is always a subtle problem with wanting to rely on the written word.

Firstly, there is the belief that writing only came in with the Romans, it's one that's still very prevalent and fits well with the mistaken concept that our prehistoric ancestors were 'savages' whose lives were 'nasty, brutish and short'. This belief began to be knocked down in the 1960s but is still the one most people hold and is a big problem as it stands there in the way of reality. It makes me think of Pink Floyd's wonderful song One More Brick in the Wall ... and Merlin (whilst possibly approving of Floyd) is not about walls, in fact just the opposite. He's about doorways and thresholds.

Then there is the problem of the survival of the written word. We in Britain live in a wet, boggy country, many parts of which have acid soil, so unless things are written on stone they do not survive ... and when was the last time you chiselled out a letter on a piece of stone? But absence of evidence is not evidence of absence. Because writing may not have survived in our climate, and evidence of it certainly has not yet been discovered, that does not mean we didn't do it.

We really do not know what our prehistoric ancestors wrote down, or if they did, or on what they might have written, or when they began to do writing. Paper is very easy to make, we used to do it in primary school, but it doesn't last a day if you leave it out in the rain; similarly, we used to make inks at school and they disappear like nobody's business in the wet. Even birch-bark and animal hide doesn't last long in our soggy climate. Most of the ancient writing that has been found has come from dry desert-type places and/or has been carefully preserved in dry

13

caves or stone buildings.

Our folk lived in very nice roundhouses – having stayed for some time in a reconstructed one I can attest they're great. They're also ecologically sound in that they go back to nature pretty quickly once you stop living in them ... along with things like paper and bark and skins. Ask any archaeologist about finding evidence for even an Anglo-Saxon roundhouse, and they are only in the region of 1,500 years old. They'll roll their eyes and tell you the best they usually find is post-hole marks in the soil to show a pit that has now been filled up with soil similar to what is around it, and so very hard to see. Our Mesolithic ancestors (a mere 7,000-12,000 years ago) lived in what we might now call 'benders' so there really isn't going to be much to find, is there? Star Carr, for instance, the place of the stunning deer masks, has been a wonderful addition to our scanty knowledge of those times, and has helped us understand the fascinating and complex society of Doggerland a little better, but has not been able to throw any light at all on our writing skills.

So what I'm saying is that just because the only written evidence of Merlin that scholars have so far found is only 1,000 to 1,500 years old does not mean that that is when someone 'invented' Merlin. He's ancient, very ancient, and was never *invented*. Our ancestors, way back, knew him intimately. They likely called him by different names to the Merlin we know, indeed in the old Brythonic tongue his name would be Myrddin – which you say as Murthin. This can all be rather troublesome if you like a tidy life, and that could well be part of why our modern idea of Merlin gets so dumbed down. Merlin is complex, non-linear and it's just not possible to put him in a box.

He lives in our tales as well as in nature but, unfortunately, the academic fraternity tend to disparage these tales, telling us they have nothing to do with history and so are not 'true'. Well, most of the time otherworld doesn't have anything to do with 'history' as it is taught in schools and universities either, it just isn't useful.

Merlin is spirit. He's not *about* spirit, he actually *is* it, as are all of our old and supposedly lost gods in Britain. He and they are otherworldly beings; they are not about history in the everyday meaning of the word.

Like so many things, the word history itself has been dumbed down and reduced in scope by the cramped, organised world most people call normality nowadays. It wasn't always like this and, indeed, it's only over the past 2,000 years that it has become so and most especially since the so-called Age of Enlightenment and the Industrial Revolution. The Age of Enlightenment had its good points (like Beethoven) and its bad points like the various philosophers who did quite a good job of *reducio ad abserdam*, reducing the old wisdom to absurdity, through their misconceptions of both the natural world and how people work/think. Very little of what they propose has anything to do with reality and only works when everyone agrees to accept their rules. They did their best to reduce the old ways of Mother Earth to superstition.

If we look at synonyms for the word 'history' we have narration, record, story, chronicle, saga and memoir, just to mention a few. These are not words that immediately come to most people's minds but they are good ones. The tales of Merlin are all of these things – story, chronicle, saga and even memoir – but they certainly do not come under the guise of linear history as it is taught nowadays, and nor should they for that's not their purpose. They're not about a set of 'facts' that follow along in chronological order, and have been put together by a coterie of people who view those facts in that particular light, and who also wish to propound them to others and so increase the set of believers. Yes, I most certainly am a cynic! Most of us know the terms 'rewriting history' and 'history is always written by the winners', but we tend to forget those useful aphorisms when presented with a historian with alphabet soup after her or his name and an authoritative manner. We should hang onto them; they keep us rooted in reality.

Merlin in Books

If you'd like to read more about Merlin I've put a bibliography at the end. You'll see it contains both non-fiction and fiction. It really isn't a good idea to separate these two so rigorously, take both together and they give you many insights into reality rather than just conformist history.

My personal favourite books include those by John Matthews, who has done excellent personal and scholarly work on Merlin. His book *Merlin: Shaman, Prophet, Magician* is a good place to begin. John Matthews and his wife Caitlin are well known in Celtic circles in Britain and I find their work extremely useful.

Another author I find very valuable is Jean Markale, particularly his *Merlin: Priest of Nature*. Jean Markale was a Breton writer, poet, and radio show host as well as a lecturer and high school French teacher, who had very strong connections with Merlin. Markale is considered controversial and gets short shrift from academics who often follow more *normative* and conservative methods and, in consequence, they tend to balk at what he says. Additionally, they don't like his interest in the occult nor his work with Carl Jung's concept of collective unconscious. I trained in Transpersonal Psychology, and in Jung's work, so this is home territory for me and makes a lot of sense. I gather that the vast majority of non-Jungian psychologists still don't accept the concept of the collective, which I find quite sad, especially for their clients.

T. H. White's story *The Once and Future King* is another good source. No, it's not academic, it's fiction, but it gives the idea, the concept, and the essence of Merlin very well. It shows him as the shapeshifter, as the wize-ard, the wise one; it shows how he teaches and how he learns for himself too. This comes out especially well in the story of Merlin's battle with the wizardess, which is a wonderful one for shapeshifting, showing how each of them chooses their change to try to thwart the other – Merlin wins with a wonderful trick! I often wonder if White was a shaman himself as he tells it all so well.

Another taleweaver who has a very good angle on Merlin is Mary Stewart in her trilogy, *The Crystal Cave*, *The Hollow Hills* and *The Last Enchantment*. These, for me, give insights into other aspects of Merlin that are not usually shown in the stories and histories. Her version certainly holds close to the truths of one, at least, of his many incarnations.

R. J. Stewart's books are worth reading too. He is another controversial writer who has studied most of the written lore on Merlin and has his own take on it. I find him useful and interesting.

Geoffrey of Monmouth is one of the best known of the Norman writers who has worked Merlin's stories. Geoffrey's *Historia Regum Britanniae*, which he wrote around 1136, is an amalgamation of the characters of Myrddin Wyllt and Myrddin Emrys. He tried to tell them as 'real history' which, I suspect, has confused many academics into thinking that we ignorant folk believed all this was 'real' in an everyday sense. That's quite wrong. We old ones have always known how the stories walk between the worlds, they are allegorical and metaphorical and show us how things are ... but not in a modern everyday concrete way.

Myrddin Wyllt was said to be a North Brythonic prophet who was thought to be mad. He lived in the Caledonian Forest, under an apple tree, with a pig. The apple tree and the pig have lots of connections to our old stories, in particular to the Apple Isle, Avalon, of which one of the physical manifestations is Lundy Island off the coast from Appledore and near where I was brought up. Another is Ynys Enlli or Bardsey Island, which is one of the places Merlin retired to at the end of his life. The pig connects to Ceridwen, one of whose totems is the Great White Sow. The white sow connects to Dyfrig who is the Merlin figure from where I currently live – but more of him later. It's all incredibly complex, twisted and twined together, not simple or linear at all. And this Merlin, Myrddin Wyllt, is not supposed to have had any connection to King Arthur.

Myrddin Emrys, on the other hand, was said to be the son of the Romano-British war leader Ambrosius Aurelianus and had all the strong connections to Arthur we most of us know about. He's the Merlin on which Mary Stewart based her hero in her Merlin Trilogy.

Out of these two figures – Myrddin Wyllt and Myrddin Emrys – Geoffrey of Monmouth made a composite figure who he called Merlin Ambrosius, which is the Latinised version of Myrddin Emrys. This is the wizard of the Arthurian saga on which many modern films and TV series are based. Geoffrey says this Merlin is buried near Paimpont in the Forest of Broceliande, in Brittany, which ties him up with the Merlin of the Breton legends. Geoffrey was certainly trying to make a General Theory of Everything out of his tale! He hasn't succeeded any more than the scientists have (as yet) done in their struggle to put everything together. Both Merlin and the universe require us to go a lot further in complexity and integration than we've managed so far. But Geoffrey's story is what many historians now base their ideas of Merlin on and it really has made a mixed-scraps-pudding of him. It was written for one of the first romantic audiences (the early Normans) and cut-n-styled to fit them so it's really not sensible to rely on it too heavily. It has made excellent material for Hollywood films though.

Robert de Boron, who wrote in the late 11th and early 12th centuries, a bit after Geoffrey of Monmouth, is another of the Norman writers who gives us his view of Merlin. He tells a lot about Merlin's power to shapeshift and his *Prose Merlin* contains many instances of it and also tells us about Merlin's connection to the Holy Grail. And Robert shows us he has a playful, teasing and witty personality, which makes a lot of sense as we Britons can be worse than Zen for riddling and teasing, and wit is a natural gift that comes with the cornflakes.

If you want poetry maybe your best bet is the Victorian poet Tennyson. His *Idylls of the King* is his most famous version of the Arthurian stories, but a quick word of advice here ... try reading it to yourself aloud! The *sounds* of the words were as meaningful and as much a part of the whole thing as the meanings of the words for the Victorians. Sound in poetry is meaningful like in music and in those days poetry was often read aloud and intended to be so.

3

Shapeshifting

Merlin is a shifter. All ancient wise ones are shifters, it comes with the territory (and the cornflakes!).

Shifting is partly about perception, how you are perceived ... and how you wish to be perceived. Merlin makes sure you perceive him in the manner that will most quickly attract your attention and help you understand what he's trying to show and/or tell you. This is what we all try to do as awenyddion (shamans); we try to make ourselves part of the message in a way that will help our audience understand. Shapeshifting is about appearing in the way that will:

- Enable your audience to hear what you say and not reject you
- Entice them to come where they need to be because they just cannot or will not see it for themselves
- Scare the shit out of them so they can hear and understand better!

As we see from his stories, Merlin uses all of these tactics to reach us, and probably a few more as well.

Here are some of the shapes he assumes from the Arthurian tales:

- A woodcutter with an axe hanging round his neck, big shoes, a torn coat, bristly hair, and a large beard
- Another time one of Uther's followers finds him up in the Northumberland forest shifted into an ugly man who tends a great herd of beasts
- At yet another time he appears as a handsome man and

then as a beautiful boy

- Much later in the stories he comes to Arthur as a tall, black, bristly and fierce peasant wearing leather boots, a wool coat, a hood, and a belt of knotted sheepskin
- Eventually he appears as an old, short hunchback with a long beard, in an old and torn woollen coat, carrying a club, and driving a great herd of beasts before him.

I love these descriptions ... and they are all links to our old gods and particularly to Custennin who is Lord of the Beasts, carries a club and tends a herd of all the beasts of the Earth. Jean Markale calls Merlin a *priest of nature* and so he is.

The Custennin role is one he loves to play with folk who might be a bit posh, have a them-and-us attitude, are stand-offish and consider themselves better than others. Thinking yourself better than other folk is not an evolutionary attitude in Merlin's books and evolution of the spirit is what Merlin wants. The ability to ask, listen to, and work-with all Nature is what he needs from us ... and what we need to learn from him too.

Merlin also shifts into the form of beasts, particularly stags as he has a very strong relationship with deer. In the *Livre d'Artus*, Robert de Boron tells how Merlin enters Rome in the form of a huge stag with one white fore-foot. He bursts into the presence of Julius Caesar to tell him that only the wildman of the woods can interpret the dream that has been troubling the emperor. Later, he returns to Caesar as a shaggy black man, barefoot and with a torn coat – the Custennin figure again.

In this story Merlin shifts to try to get through to Caesar. Both the stag and the wildman are about the deep, ancient wisdom of nature; he is trying to show the emperor the arrogance in thinking he can do without nature, or that he can control it to give him what he wants. Julius Caesar is the Roman who began the changes that led to us old ones living in hiding. This Merlin story is how he tells Caesar that he's got it wrong, that he cannot understand his dream until he makes his peace with nature. Fortunately, none of us were holding our breath at that time, 2,000 years ago, as Caesar never even made the attempt to make his peace with nature, or us.

In another version of the story, Merlin goes into the forest of Brocéliande in Brittany (one of his more well-known haunts) and there he transforms himself into the giant herdsman, Custennin. This time he is huge, hideous, bent, black, lean, hairy and old, with a hump on his back; his hair and ears hang down to his waist, while his head is as big as a buffalo's and his hands and feet are on backwards. As before, he carries a club, but this time he wears a wolf-skin and leggings and, again, he calls a herd of deer to come and graze around him.

Merlin shifts into a twisted, deformed shape. His hands and feet are on backwards, he's hunchbacked while his ears and head are vastly out of proportion – what is this about? Is he showing how nature has been deformed by human greed, by Caesar's wish to conquer? Is he trying to awaken his listeners to stop the harm they're doing? The description says he's hideous – perhaps because people have made him so and he is trying to awaken them?

Merlin, in his Custennin role and in the story with Caesar, reminds me very much of the Lady Ragnall who appears to Arthur in a similar guise in the story Ragnall's Wedding. Arthur has just killed a deer when he should not have done, he sees her and says, '*You are awful! I see in your face the face of every beast in the world. Your eyes are owl's eyes; your nose, a cat's nose; your ears, lion's ears; your teeth are wolf's teeth; your hands are bear's claws and your feet are the hooves of goats. Your legs are like tree roots; your body is gnarled like the trunk of the World Tree and your arms are knotted branches. Your breasts are great hills and mountains and your belly and hips are big enough to birth the world!*'

Ragnall replies, '*I am Ragnall, the owl who passes across the face of the moon and causes all who see me to shiver. I am mistress of the beasts. I hold within me all creatures and give them succour. Any man who harms a beast, harms me! Any man who harms a plant, a flower or a tree, harms me!'*

Merlin is Lord of the Beasts as Ragnall is their lady. This is how it is in our old ways, always the masculine and the feminine are entwined, the one holding the other in their difference and in their sameness. He appears as a deer, a stag, and he has deer around him. Ragnall helps Arthur after he has offended the Lord of the Summer's Day (another name for the Lord of the Forest and the Beasts) by killing a deer for which he had not asked permission.

Both Matthews and Markale draw out this side of him, Lord of the Animals and Lord of Nature, and this is very much my own experience too. I mostly see him either in the natural world or showing me some aspect of it that I need to know.

But there's even more to shapeshifting than assuming an appearance, the shape or form of something or someone else, like becoming a stag or a wildman as he does in these stories. It's much deeper than that. This little tale of one of my own experiences of shapeshifting will give you an idea of what I'm talking about.

Way back in the 1980s I was working with a friend who also taught the old ways. She'd been telling us about being, becoming and appearing invisible, and how useful it is in the ordinary everyday world. *'It's partly about wearing a cloak, but it's also about hiding your essence. Look, I'll show you,'* she said. With that she asked us to be very quiet for a moment as she prepared then she asked someone near the door to let her dog, a lovely Doberman, into the room. The person did so and the dog trotted in, very glad to be with us as he was sometimes allowed to be. Then he sniffed, looked up and began to whine. He trotted round the circle, passing his mistress, and sniffing the whole time while looking about and whining. At last he stopped in the midst of the circle, sat down and gave a long, low, miserable howl. That was too much! My friend dropped her cloak of invisibility immediately and the dog ran straight to her, yelping and fussing and rubbing himself against her. Finally, he stood up with his paws on her shoulders to lick her face.

Everyone got it, just like that we got it, as I hope you have too! Nobody can say anyone was fooling anyone as the dog had no concept of placebos and other such human ideas. He wanted his mistress, he knew she should be in the room but, when he came in, he could find no sign of her. Remember the sniffing? It wasn't just sight and her form she cloaked, but her whole essence including her scent. She changed her whole self as well so she was truly no longer in the room – despite that we could all see her form. The dog could not sense her in any way or find any evidence of her in the room. She was not there, not as far as he could tell.

But as soon as she dropped her cloak of invisibility he saw her.

For us who had seen the whole process she didn't disappear, we still saw the shadow-form of her, but the dog who had not seen the process knew she – her essence – was not there. My Dad taught me this way as a child and I've used it all my life, at school when I didn't want to do sports, coming home on the tube in London, past midnight, and having to walk through a rough neighbourhood, even when I didn't want my husband to see me once (and no, it was nothing horrid!).

When people see someone as something, or someone, else this is because the person has cloaked their true *essence* within a form that they have imagined. To go deeper, as my friend did with her dog, you need to change your inner-self, your essence, as well.

Working with Illusion

One of the things Merlin loves to show and teach us is how to discern between reality and illusion. There are all sorts of levels of illusion from the gestalt and Rorschach stuff where you see an image as something other than it is, to seeing mirages, seeing

clouds as animals and cities, whole landscapes in cloud forma-
tions, to the illusions politicians, ad men and businesses try on,
which we often call 'spin'.

Most of us do shifting every day in a very simple way ... we
put on a suit, or a uniform, or some special clothes, to go to work
... we change our form. We become, shift into, the 'work person'
and when we come home we change and become, shift into, the
home person, we may even take a shower or bath to 'clean off the
dust of the day'. This is ritual stuff although most of us don't
think of it as such, including the ritual cleaning. We *become* the
work person in looks and manners in order to be able to do our
job. It's a form of shapeshifting.

People who work with wildlife camouflage themselves so they
are not so easily seen by the wildlife they want to watch, that too
includes their scent such as rolling in mud or even shit, and
definitely *not* wearing perfumes and deodorants that will tell any
self-respecting rabbit who and what they are from a mile off!

Wildlife workers may also be able to call animals and birds to
them, sometimes by making the same call as the bird or animal
makes in particular circumstances. I once got a raven really cross
at the Tower of London by making raven noises! He could hear a
new raven, but not see it, so he stomped up and down on top of
the arch to the White Tower *caarking* crossly until he eventually
traced the sound to me when he glared very hard and then flew
off. It was funny, but also stunningly amazing to *feel* myself
talking with this bird. I can do it with owls too. My Uncle Jack
was a wizard at calling hawks and falcons, but he never needed
to use his voice, he could transmit to them directly which is a
whole other thing and not to do with illusion as making bird-calls
is.

Essence Work

But there is more to shapeshifting ... it's not only about shifting
your form, but also about shifting your essence.

Merlin was friend to my Uncle Jack as well as my Dad. Jack and Dad had their own ways of communicating with nature and learned them with Merlin's help. They and Merlin taught me and I passed that on to my husband, Paul, as I do to my students too. We all need to expand our ability to connect with everything non-human, learning to do that expands our whole outlook on life, the universe and everything, we no longer look at the non-human world as objects for our pleasure and profit, we see everything as at least equal to ourselves. When we do that we know in our bones that we must care for and respect everything, our attitudes change and we no longer harm the Earth, which suits Merlin down to the socks!

A priest of nature is very well able to communicate with all the animal, vegetable and mineral kingdoms as well humans, and this requires that you are able to *sense into the essence* of other creatures, plants and rocks. Another of our famous shamans, Taliesin, is well known for being able to be everything, as he shows us in his poem that begins, *'I am a stag: of seven tines ...'* Merlin, too, is able to **be** everything for this is the ultimate quality of shapeshifting.

If you want to be a stag, a cat, a salmon, an eagle, or a tree, mountain, or a wave of the sea, then you must experience its essence, know what it is to **be** that thing. You can't do it by reading a book! Even a weekend course won't help unless it's completely experiential and probably quite a bit scary! One of my early teachers, one of the old women of the village, told me that if I really wanted to become awenydd (shaman in the old British tongue) then I must learn how to become a worm, a cloud, a cat, a rat ... everything. She emphasised that I couldn't just choose nice, pretty, comfy things, but I must also learn the difficult, painful and scary ones too. Students can find that to be a big stumbling block. But what is it about?

Everything in the cosmos is *animate*, i.e. it has spirit, its own essence. The word anima, which is the root of animate, comes from a word for breath. Anima is the spirit that enables our bodies to live.

When I was at university, Merlin told me the story of how the spirit incarnates. 'After all the chat and parties with your friends, the others in your totem group,' he began, 'when you've decided the sort of life that will suit the job you've promised to do next time around, and agreed it with your parents-to-be, then you have to get down to making it happen. All that agreement gets fixed at your conception. So your spirit, your essence – the part of you that's really able to see me – goes to the store and tells the person behind the counter that you're about to incarnate on Earth. The store-person says, 'OK. Then you'll be needing some physical matter, some feelings-stuff and some thinking-matter to make your spacesuit for living on Planet Earth. Have you asked her for this?' And you have, of course.'

Merlin looked down his nose at me and grinned. I nodded back. I knew that everything you want you need to ask for, it's the first lesson in the old ways that we all learn.

'Right,' Merlin continued, 'so the store-person goes and gets you the physical materials, the emotions-feelings and the thinking stuff you need to make your spacesuit. You take the parcels...' 'Saying thanks,' I interrupted him. 'Yes, saying thanks,' he went on. 'Then you dive into your mother's womb, with the parcels of goodies, and help her begin the building of you.' He paused. 'So ... do you see that you're most certainly not the physical personality that is Elen for this lifetime?'

'Yes, I do,' I said. 'I'm a spirit who's wearing a spacesuit for Planet Earth. And it's currently called Elen.'

'That's right. But ... did you know you can, and do, change the quality of that essence, your spirit, as you live through each incarnation? And that doing that also changes the physical stuff you've borrowed from Planet Earth for your spacesuit. Did you realise that?'

That gave me pause. Up to then I'd thought that one's spirit was one's spirit, sort of set in stone. What Merlin had just said showed me that that wasn't the case at all. 'So ...' I was thinking aloud now, '... so, I change the stuff of the Earth, the stuff I've borrowed, by how I live?' Merlin nodded. 'And how I live also changes my spirit?' Merlin nodded again. 'Hmmm!' I sank back into thought. That was pretty big stuff. The more I thought about it the more responsibility I felt. After a few more moments Merlin began to chuckle.

'You look as if you'd just discovered a huge rock that you somehow have to push up a hill,' he said.

'That's about how I feel!' I agreed.

'It does come as a bit of a shock, at first,' he said, 'but you've already been doing it for 21 years of this life without really noticing, so just how bad is it?'

That made me laugh. 'I suppose I have! But now I wonder how knowing this stuff, about helping to make myself for the incarnation, is going to make me act in future.'

'More consciously, I hope!' he retorted. 'Not that you've been ditzing around all that much, but everyone can use being on top of their game during their life. Knowing how you began it is helpful, it changes how you look at things, and how you do things.'

'And,' he added, 'realising that how you act changes the matter-stuff you borrowed from the Earth, and that means that when you give it back, when you die and no longer have any use for the spacesuit you've made, you give it back to her in a more evolved condition than it was when you first got it ... hopefully!' He was grinning now.

Somehow I managed to smile back. That was another big one and it prompted a further thought. 'You mean, that's sort of healing the Earth?'

'That is how we can heal the Earth,' he said. 'All the ceremonies and candles and flowers and singing and stuff, they only have any effect if the people doing them are *also* working to evolve themselves. If they're not it's just sugar-candy. They have to really be doing it, making changes in how they think, and how they use their emotions, and how they live physically. When you die you give back the matter you borrowed from the Earth in a better, or worse, state than it was when you got it before your birth. If it's worse, because you lived uncaringly, then you've messed up the Earth too.'

I'm still thinking about that, forty-plus years later. I think about it every day. And it hurts quite a lot because I can see the effects of people living uncaringly all around me. Another thing Merlin reminded me of was the old Taoist saying, *'You cannot change anything but yourself. But, in changing yourself, you see the world change around you.'* It's true. And it does help. You live your life to the very best you can, asking all the time for the help of your spirit friends both those in incarnation like the trees and flowers and bees in your garden, and those not currently in incarnation like your familiar spirits, teachers and the rest of your otherworldly gang.

Learning to live as best I can has included learning to be a worm, a beetle, a moth, a blowfly, a snake, a cockroach, and all the things people tend to go 'ugh!' and recoil from, as well as the pretty foxes and trees. If I exclude the things that I feel are horrid then I exclude a part of Life, and I exclude the spirit that inhabits everything. If I do that then I have no chance at all of being awenydd, being spirit-keeper. Everything has its own spirit, its own essence – my cats, each of the trees in the garden, all the plants, and the animals who visit the garden too, the foxes, badgers, hedgehogs, falcons and hawks, the little songbirds, the mice and voles. The hills and mountains on my skyline have their own essence, and the village where I grew up, the river near where I live, my home herself, my car even. Everything.

So I learned to communicate with the creature or plant I wished to experience, and to ask them if they would be so kind as to allow me within them to feel what it's like. To give you a quick example of what it's like, this little story of me and my cat may help.

I was lying in bed very early one summer morning, listening to the dawn chorus, when I felt my little ginger cat, Goldy, calling me. She was my familiar spirit for her incarnation and is still around now she's passed the job on to Izzy and gone over the rainbow bridge.

'Hi,' she said, 'it's great out here. Want to come?' I said yes at once and asked her if I might come inside her and share her essence. 'Come ahead,' she replied. The next instant I was within her and seeing out of her eyes, which was a bit weird as cat-vision isn't like ours. Everything appeared rather like a wide-angle lens around the edges and I could see further round the side of my head than I can as a human while, at the same time, the centre of my vision where I focused was pin-sharp and better than my normal human vision. She was hunkered down in the long grass of next-door's garden, the grass stems looking thick and going right over our head. I say *our* head because there really were two of us in there, both me and her.

She got up and prowled towards an old oil-tin, it looked huge from this perspective, but the human bit of me/us could still read the old label on the side so I knew it wasn't really the height of a house. It was strange and wonderful to feel how her body moved too. She was very fit and lithe. At that time, I was still doing jazz dance with my friend at the Pineapple Centre in Covent Garden, London, so I was very fit and lithe too ... but nothing like Goldy! She was an order of magnitude, at least, better than me.

We prowled into the oil tin. It was damp and muddy inside and there Goldy saw a worm. She ate it! So, of course, I ate it too! That was really weird ... from Goldy's perspective it was delicious, from mine it was disgusting! She sort of internally stared at me with a 'for goodness sake' expression, while I was grimacing and doing my best not to choke as it would affect her throat and she was enjoying it. She gave the cat-equivalent of a disgusted snort and took us out of the tin and up a tree.

I don't have a good head for heights. She did. So that was incredible too. This time I found I was with her, happy and had lost my fear, but unfortunately that didn't last when I came back to my human body. But it was great to be looking down (still with that very different vision) onto the ground twenty feet below us, and be able to see the tiniest movements of little insects as well as a mouse who was hunting through the grass.

After a while I thanked Goldy and left her down in next-door's garden to come back to my bed. I lay there a long while, pondering over my journey with her.

That experience is what I mean by knowing in our bones. We experience the reality of being another creature, something other than ourselves. I've used human-speak to tell you what Goldy spoke with me but, of course, it wasn't like that. It all happens instantaneously, like thought in a way but even more than that. We communicated by a sort of 'knowing', kenning again, that didn't need human words.

That's shapeshifting at a deep level. It's something we can all learn to do and Merlin will help us with the learning.

4

Dragons, Demons and the Fatherless Child

Dragons and demons are deep in Merlin's stories. And so is being a 'fatherless' child.

Vortigern and the Dragons

One of the best known Merlin stories is his contretemps with Vortigern. Vortigern had an important stronghold not far from where I now live, at a place called Ganarew in our little kingdom of Ergyng. In English it's called Little Doward, an amazing place and very magical, I work there quite often by myself and with my students. The stories say it's the place of Vortigern's downfall, where Ambrosius – who Mary Stewart uses as the possible father of Merlin in *The Crystal Cave* – burned down the wooden castle on the tall hill with Vortigern inside. The story of Merlin and the dragons and Vortigern didn't happen there but much further west at a mountain that's now called Dinas Emrys.

One of the names Merlin is known by is Emrys, its Latinisation is Ambrosius, his father's name, and means 'light'; *dinas* means city in Welsh. Dinas Emrys – city of light – is a little, rocky, wooded hillock only 250ft high, near Beddgelert in Gwynedd, up by Snowdon. The Glaslyn river runs at its foot and it overlooks the southern end of the lake, Llyn Dinas, lake of the city. It's worth thinking about the word 'city'. In English it means a town that becomes a city by charter and usually contains a cathedral; to go deeper and before towns had charters or cathedrals, it suggests a significant sacred site. Dinas Emrys is certainly that.

The story of Vortigern's tower and the dragons is full of meaning and insights but, like all of our stuff, you have to stalk and hunt and search for them. The old ones and the ancestors never give away anything easily, we have to work, show our commitment and persistence.

Vortigern's Welsh name is Guorthigirn and later Gwrtheyrn. It is Gildas and Bede who gave him to us as Vortigern and Vortigern is actually a title, a job-description. In old Breton they would say *machtiern*, and in Cornish *myghtygern*, both of which mean pledge-chief. Both Breton and Cornish are versions of our old Brythonic language.

Vortigern's character is very complex. He was a Briton who took a Saxon wife and came to an agreement with the Saxon invaders, which many disliked. He was warlord of much of southern Britain and invited the Saxon brothers Hengist and Horsa, with three keels (shiploads) of Saxons, to come to Britain to help him keep back the Picts. The Saxons came, but then there were all sorts of arguments over their 'payment in kind', meaning the land Vortigern had promised them. Vortigern's backsliding made the Saxons somewhat cross so they devastated the land. Vortigern fled to Wales, to escape his own people's vengeance as much as run from the Saxons, and decided to build himself a strong tower at Dinas Emrys.

The story then goes that each day Vortigern's men would work to build the tower but the next morning they would return to find the masonry all collapsed in a heap overnight. This continued for some weeks until Vortigern's advisors (sometimes called druids) told him to seek out a young boy not conceived by a mortal man, the fatherless child. He sent his men out across the land to find such a lad and the boy they found was called Myrddin Emrys – his name possibly means 'sea fortress of light'. The advisors told Vortigern he must kill the boy and sprinkle his blood on the foundations in order to appease the spirits of the hill so they would allow him to build his tower. When Merlin was brought to Vortigern and told what the advisors had said, he laughed, scorning this advice, and told Vortigern that the tower could not stand because beneath it there was a hidden pool in which lived two dragons (wyrms). Every night they rose up and fought, and their rising made the tower fall down.

The dragon story has its roots in the ancient story of Lludd and Llefelys, sons of the sun god Beli. On every May Eve, King Lludd of Britain heard a hideous scream. No-one knew whence this scream came and it so frightened the people that it caused infertility, panic and mayhem throughout the land. Lludd sought help from his brother Llefelys, King of Brittany, who told him the scream was caused by two battling dragons. The British dragon (the red one, now on the Welsh banner) would scream when it feared it was being defeated by the alien white dragon. Lludd captured both dragons in a cauldron filled with mead – one of our 'medicines', like for example peyote for other cultures – which they drank. They then transformed themselves (as apparently dragons did) into pigs, and fell asleep. Lludd wrapped them in a white silk cloth and laid their sleeping forms in the now empty cauldron under Dinas Emrys.

Merlin told Vortigern it was these dragons who had awoken, transformed back to dragon-shape and now fought each night to make a ruin of Vortigern's tower. He explained that the red dragon represented the British people while the white dragon was the Saxon invaders he had brought into the country, and who were now laying it waste while he did nothing to stop them. Merlin called and the two beasts rose up and began to fight. The red dragon slew the white one which Merlin translated as the overthrow, in due course, of the Saxons and the subsequent demise of Vortigern. The druid advisors had warned him that the fatherless boy must also be slain because he was a danger to the king and, in a sense, he was because he foretold Vortigern's end and the reason for it.

After their battle the dragons disappeared and Vortigern went on to build his tower successfully although to no purpose in the end. He let Merlin go – not that I think he could have kept him even if he'd wanted to! The tower didn't help Vortigern so he returned to Doward where Merlin's foster-father, Emrys Wledig (Ambrosius Aurelianus), besieged it and then killed him by burning down the Ganarew fortress. The word *wledig* means *of the land* and is a title given to kings, lords, guardians of our lands; it has the same meaning as the Latin word *paganus* from which the word pagan comes, which also means of the land.

So what is all this about? Lludd and Llefelys are god-kings, sons of one of the primeval father-gods, who are guardians of the land. When things go wrong and the dragons fight the land is shaken; when they are put back to sleep then the land is able to regenerate. It's the old Wasteland story in another form. Merlin knows that kings are guardians of the land, the goddess, and that they promise to guard it all their lives; this is the pledge of the pledge-chief. Vortigern, as pledge-chief, fails in his kingly duties so Merlin shows him his end.

The sleeping dragons guard the land, and they are its watchdogs too. When Vortigern fails to guard the land they rise up, trying to show him what he's doing wrong, but he will not see. Then Merlin comes, calls the dragons and predicts Vortigern's end. The dragons go back to sleep and the land is able to be easy once more.

The Fatherless Child

According to the Christian stories, Merlin's mother lay with a demon, an otherworldly spirit, who fathered him upon her. For us old ones, this is a wonderful and good thing, we're accustomed to working with spirits and sometimes having children with them, but it was (and still is) terrifying and horrible to Christians. They attempted to make Merlin good in their eyes – realising they couldn't eradicate him from our minds – by baptising him and calling his father evil. That reinterpretation of the story is rather horrific to those of us of the old ways. The legend of the village where I now live is another version of the story of Merlin, the fatherless child, as you will see in the next chapter.

The Christian idea is that demons include the fairies, sprites and all the Faer folk, and are bad, evil things, unclean spirits, sometimes fallen angels, or spirits that will possess a person and need to be exorcised. Western occultism and Renaissance magic went further and believed a demon is a spiritual entity that may be conjured and controlled.

The latter makes my head reel. Summoning a spirit and wanting to control it is anathema to our old ways, although some witches do practise it. The subjugation and control of another creature – spirit or material – is not something we do, so the concept of a spirit controlling a human, or vice versa, is a non sequitur. It's not possible. Humans can and do achieve control over *thoughtforms*, i.e. a creature made from the thoughts of a human being, but these are *not* spirits although they may appear spirit-like to the inexperienced. They are created by and from the persistent, often obsessive, thoughts of either themselves or another human.

Merlin's father was definitely not a thoughtform.

The theologians called the demons who slept with people incubi, the male spirits, and succubi, the female ones. The word incubus comes from the Latin word *incubo*, which means a sexual or sensual dream-happening induced by a demon and the incubus, or demon or devil.

But the Night Mare is an ancient reality for us, we've had stories of visitations by night spirits since time out of mind. And we celebrate the queen of the night spirits, the Mari Lwyd, on her feast day soon after the midwinter solstice. Her totem is a horse's head on a pole, which is dressed as a bride. It's carried from house to house through the village or town on either 12th Night (6th January) also called 'Old Christmas Day', or on 'Old 12th Night' (17th January).

These dates were born out of the reform of the old calendar, but we still celebrate the old days when we used to celebrate

Sun-Return, which happens now on the 25th December. It's the day the sun begins to move on again after the standstill of the solstice. If you're able to watch the sun rise on the mornings of 22nd, 23rd and 24th December you'll see that it apparently rises on the same point on the horizon for the three days – Stonehenge is, of course, a good place for this as that's part of what it was built for. We celebrate Sun-Return, the day the sun moves on again, as the beginning of the new year as from that time on there will be more light each day until midsummer, when the reverse happens. We celebrate Sun-Go-Down at midsummer, after the three-day standstill, solstice, again honouring the beginning of the lessening of the light each day until the turnaround again at midwinter.

So the Mari Lwyd is the *lady of the change of the year* who comes both as a skull and a bride, the old and the new. She chases out the old things that are past their sell-by date so leaving space for the new to come in, and she is both fearsome to chase out the old and delightful because we do all like new things and hope that the new will be good. The Night Mare is a lady of thresholds, a liminal lady who stands between the old and the new. She is a night spirit, the Night-Mare, who facilitates change, as Merlin does, and we do not fear her coming.

The fatherless child is a concept that occurs all around the world. Magical children are often born of a human woman and fathered by an otherworldly being, or sometimes (as with Merlin's partner, Vivien) they're born of an otherworldly mother and fathered by a human.

For most of our human time the fatherless child had a respected, honoured, revered and valued parentage. Then along came the Romans and the Christians and everything otherworldly became 'the devil and all his works', the otherworldly fathers became demons and the mothers were shamed. Until then, to be the mother of the fatherless child was always a wonderful and honourable thing. The fatherless child himself or herself is a magical being at once both human and otherworldly, and has extreme powers, far greater than those of humans, and the stories of Merlin show this.

Being born of both worlds, spirit and human, enables Merlin to have a continuous connection across the worlds, always in contact with both matter and spirit at the same time. It's one of the things he teaches anyone willing to work with him and learning to do this, to be a walker between worlds, is part of what all our apprentices learn. They then go on to forge their own swords of wisdom from that experience and, eventually, are able to draw the sword out of the stone and help others.

My own experience with Merlin has shown me how wonderful this connection and awareness of both otherworld and thisworld at the same time is. It's one of the most important things he has taught me but, needless to say, I'm nothing like as good as him at doing it!

5

Pig Moor: Dyfrig, Ergyng and Mynydd Myrddin

I now live in one of Merlin's birthplaces. It's in the tiny ancient kingdom of Ergyng, in the Welsh Marches, the twilight lands between Wales and England.

When we first moved out of London, back in 1999/2000, I had no conscious intention to live where I now do, not at first. In fact, I thought I was going back to Exmoor, but I was drawn, pulled and chivvied to come here by one of those 'somethings' we all get from time to time. I didn't know, not until about a month after I'd moved in here, about any Merlin connections and then it all began to fall on me – in the case of one book, quite literally!

This is quite normal on the path of the old British ways; other-world probably feels it's worse than herding kittens to get us to do what they need of us and easier to get us to do things when we don't properly know what we're doing. Those of us who walk this path are mostly strong characters with lots of ideas, person-ality and likely attitude too, so we often feel we can improve on their instructions. Ha! In this instance they carefully herded me towards living here by making places I'd originally preferred unavailable and, finally, getting me here to look at the place. That made a big difference. The things I need most are seclusion and quiet, with no humans around for at least half a mile, a well of good spring water, a large garden, lots of wildlife, and enough room so I don't have to see my husband all day if I don't want to. Oh and a really safe place for my cats! This place has all of those. And then I saw the ley line that runs through the middle of the house … that was the clincher.

So we moved in. It felt good and the spirits of place – of the house, the garden, and the small woodland next door, and the spirits of the stream and the fields too – all welcomed me, guardedly of course at first as they wanted to check me out, see who I was and become sure of me before they came to a decision. But the welcome feel was there as soon as I saw the place. We moved in and I began to get to know them as I sat with them, listening to what the garden spirit wanted me to do to turn the garden into what she needed and wanted. That was the beginning.

After about a month I went into town for a wander around, to get to know the place a bit instead of just doing grocery shopping and essentials. I popped into the local map shop; I love maps and this one was very good. I was standing looking at walking-maps of the area when a book fell off the shelf onto my head. After a grumbled 'ouch!' I picked it up and saw the title *Arthurian Links with Herefordshire* by a local woman called Mary Andere. I began to read it, there in the shop, and after several minutes knew I had to have it so I bought it, came home and was un-talkable-to for hours while I read it. It was the beginning of knowing where I'd landed – in one of the places where the Merlin was born.

Merlin is a far deeper and further-reaching figure than the person commonly portrayed on TV or in films, or even in many stories. He gets dumbed-down and simplified and restricted into being 'real' and 'historical'. Unfortunately, academics, film-makers and Uncle-Tom-Cobley-and-All, all attempt to cut Merlin to size so he will fit into their boxes, fit with their views, they cut off his toes and heels as Cinderella's sisters did to try to fit their feet into the glass slipper, and attempt to cripple him. But Merlin is *not* an historical figure in the way that, say, Queen Elizabeth I is, and most certainly doesn't fit in anyone's box. To attempt to make him do so is to completely lose the point of him. He turns up everywhere, all over Britain, in Brittany and other parts of France as well, he's a very well-travelled spirit. But that is what he is, a spirit who appears in all sorts guises, under many names, and in many places within the stories of the Celtic peoples throughout Europe.

And here was me, in the shadowy lands of the Welsh Marches, in Merlin's land. He drew me to live here so he could show me his places, all within a circle of about 20 miles around this house. Being here, working here with him, has opened up a whole new volume of my life, enabling me-the-writer.

Dyfrig of Ergyng

In this country he's known as Dyfrig of Ergyng.

Dyfrig was the son of Princess Efrddyl the daughter of King Peibio Clafrog of Ergyng.

A quick aside on pronunciation – you pronounce Dyfrig as Duvrig. You say Efrddyl as Avrthil, but I usually shorten it to Avril. Peibio Clafrog is peebeeo clavrog and clafrog means leprous.

So ... one day, Peibio came home from the wars and, as is the Celtic custom, Efrddyl washed and combed his hair and beard. As she was doing this he saw that she was heavily pregnant. 'Who is the father?' he demanded. 'I cannot tell,' she replied. He asked her again, and then a third time, and every time Efrddyl would not tell. So Peibio had her taken down to the River Wye and thrown in to drown, but the river pushed her gently back to the shore. Again Peibio threw her into the river and again the river sent her back again, and a third time she was thrown in, but the Wye would not take her and instead gave her back to her father.

Defeated by the river Peibio now had a great pyre built to see what fire would do. He set his daughter upon the bonfire to be burned to death, set light to it and went back to his home on the hill.

The next morning, he sent a servant down to the pyre to see the ashes. The servant took one look and ran straight back. 'My lord! My lord!' he panted breathlessly. 'You must come, yourself, at once.' So Peibio followed the servant down to the remains of the pyre by the river and there he found his daughter, sat upon a tall standing stone, nursing her newborn son. The place is now called Chilstone, which is a contraction of Child's Stone.

Peibio was dumbfounded. His daughter climbed down from the stone and showed him his grandson. The child reached up to touch his grandfather's cheek and straightway the leprosy was gone. Needless to say, Peibio was even more astonished, and delighted, for a new-born child that could do such a healing was well worth rearing, whoever his father might have been.

Peibio ceded the whole of the land around Madley (as it's now called) to Dyfrig. It was then was called Ynys Efrddyl, the island of Efrddyl.

Efrddyl was guardian to the waters, priestess of the sacred well and of the river, for water is the lifeblood of the land. Women of that time who were born into her position as daughter of the ruler, were usually the goddess' representative, and that was also the case with the 'saint' of the village on the edge of Exmoor where I grew up. The river Wye is the mother-water of Ergyng, and a form of the goddess, so would never take and kill her own priestess but washed her back to land. Nor would the river allow the fire to take her.

Efrddyl would not tell who the father of her child was. Her words are said to be, 'I cannot tell', and these are words that are used in several stories that relate to magical children, including Arianrhod's birthing of Dylan and Llew. It might be these words mean there was a constraint on her from otherworld not to disclose the father or maybe she didn't see him clearly because he'd shifted to a form she could not discern.

There is a great sense of trust in the story. She trusted the otherworldly shifter-father, and she trusted to the Wye, the mother-river of our place and the waters of which she was guardian, to bring her through the ordeal. Then too there is the ordeal itself. It's an initiation and a rite of passage, a threshold for both her and her son, they had to go through water and fire in order for him to be born. Fire and water are the pair of opposites at the foundation of life, like the fire and ice creation myth of the Norse people. His name, Dyfrig, means 'water baby' and that water connection makes me think again of the possible meaning of Merlin's name as sea-fortress.

In those days, mothers taught their sons, gave them everything they needed, and Efrddyl gave her son her wisdom. In his turn, Dyfrig became a teacher of the old ways he'd learned from his mother. As a young man Dyfrig found himself called to start a school down at Hennllann (Hentland) further down the Wye, which became quite famous and is mentioned in the Christian stories. But, after seven years there, he had a dream ... a beautiful woman came to him, wearing a long silver-white dress, her golden hair flowed all the way down her back and the air around her glowed golden. 'Dyfrig,' she said to him, 'you must go back up the river. Follow the Wye upstream until you come to the place where the great white sow is suckling her piglings for it is there that you must build your new school.' So Dyfrig followed the river upstream and eventually came to the place where the great white sow suckled her piglings, and there he built his most famous school.

There is a little church there now. It's on a tump (a small hill), quite a way back from where the river flows today, but you can see how the old water channel ran 1,500 years ago. There are strong energy lines twining up the nave to a vortex under the altar where they spiral together, widdershins and deosil. If you like to explore the old churches throughout Britain and Europe you'll find that just about all of them have this sort of energy-line formation. The Christians knew quite enough in the old days to build their churches where we already knew the land was special. This place was called Moch Ros, which means 'pig moor' – moch means pig and ros means moor – in honour of Ceridwen suckling her piglings there. It lies down the hill from Caer Ergyng, Peibio's stronghold, which was up on Moch Ros Ridge and not far from the Chilstone, Dyfrig's birthplace. Moch Ros is now called Moccas, which is a contraction of the old name.

Dyfrig remained at Moch Ros for the rest of his life but he did travel a lot as well. I soon found yet another connection with him. I was brought up on Exmoor and I remembered that Porlock church, on the southern bank of the Severn and the northern edge of Exmoor, is dedicated to Dyfrig. He had crossed the river and come to the land where I grew up too.

Finally, when Dyfrig grew old he chose to leave Moch Ros and go to Ynys Enlli (Bardsey Island) where he died and was buried. His feast-day is usually given as 14 Nov. Then, some 500 years later, in May 1120, the Norman lords had his body dug up and taken to Llandaff to be reburied in the cathedral there. I feel very bad about this. They dug him up to increase their own prestige instead of leaving his bones on the magical isle of Enlli where he wished them to be.

Ynys Enlli is one of the places where Merlin is said to have made his end. It's also one of the sites for the magic land of West-over-the-Sea, one of the Isles of the Faer, where Merlin took the wounded Arthur after the final battle for him to be healed.

There are many islands off the west coast of Britain and Brittany, and 'lost lands' too, all of them have claims to be lands of the Faer Folk, the wise ones and healers, places where human folk go or are taken at the time of their death. The islands are there where the sun sets into the sea, they are the sunset isles. Up in the Highlands there are islands up near Lochinver that are still called the Sunset Isles. I've been there and the idea that you could easily walk out to them is very strong, and you can certainly sail out to them. They're magical.

Christians have conflated Dyfrig into their faith although there is no reason to think he was Christian. According to their story, Dyfrig was made Bishop of Ergyng, and possibly bishop of Llandaff, and then Bishop of the whole of Glywysing and Gwent and, later still, they say he was raised to be Archbishop of Wales by St Germanus, with his base at Caerleon. As archbishop he is said to have crowned Arthur as High-King at Caer Fudi, which is thought to be Woodchester, a village in the Nailsworth Valley that runs southwards from Stroud in Gloucestershire. It's possible he was all these things for this was the time when Christianity was just beginning to work its way into our culture and there was no heavyweight attempt to convert us as yet. Christians worked alongside us in those early days and we might have grown well together, perhaps, if it hadn't been for the Augustine mission in 597AD, some 60-odd years after Dyfrig's death. The old ways continued despite the oppression this mission began but we went underground, hidden, and many of us still do stay hidden today.

As well as the local stories from here where I live, Dyfrig appears as a character in Geoffrey of Monmouth's *Historia Regum Britanniae* and Wace's *Roman de Brut*, which was based on Geoffrey's book. Much later Alfred, Lord Tennyson featured Dyfrig as a saint in his *Idylls of the King*. Even if these writers didn't really know who or what he was they realised he was important, but their stories just don't do it for me. For me and mine, Dyfrig is the son of the servant of the goddess and an other-worldly father, he is the magical child, one of our Merlin-figures, and I live in his land.

Mynydd Myrddin

About 15 miles away, down towards Abergavenny, is one of the hills under which Merlin is supposed to sleep, one of the sites of his crystal cave, and it's actually called Merlin's Mountain, Mynydd Myrddin. It's about 323m (1,060ft) high and the top gives marvellous views of the surrounding country including the dragon's back of Hay Bluff. There's a trig point half buried in the north face of a hedge, but that's not the place!

It's an interesting journey to find the actual spot, where you can reach down into the roots of the mountain. To find it you need to go beyond the hedge with the trig point and out into the field beyond where a faint path leads you into the middle of the field. If you follow it you come to a basin, a wide dip in the ground about 3m (3yds) across. When you get down into the grassy basin, and sit down, you can't see out over the edge, you're in a hollow within the top of the hill and such places have always been special for us.

John Lewis-Stempel's book *Meadowland: The Private Life of an English Field,* about the natural history of a meadow on his Herefordshire farm, gives the feel of the place. The book begins:

The Ice Moon is already rising over Merlin's Hill as I go down to the field at late evening to watch for snipe. There is real cold on the back edge of the wind, which rattles the dead tin-foil leaves left clinging on the river oaks. As I open the gate, my heart performs its usual little leap at the magnificence of the view: the great flatness of the field, its pictureframe of hedgerows, the sloping smoothness of Merlin's Hill to the left, then right around me the forbidding dam wall of the Black Mountains. There is snow along the top of the mountains, snow as smooth as wedding cake.

Sitting there, quiet and preferably alone, you can daydream. Ursula le Guin in her book *The Left Hand of Darkness* calls it *far-fetching* which, I think, is a lovely term, for we do fetch up old memories from afar, from across and between the worlds.

Mynydd Myrddin Journey

The first time I went there was nearly 20 years ago now.

I found the place, the basin in the hilltop, by reaching into the ground to touch the energy threads (as Merlin and Dad had taught me) and following them. They led me down into the dip. I sat down and closed my eyes to begin my far-fetching.

Slipping, sliding, slithering into a different consciousness, almost like Alice going down the rabbit hole, my vision flickered and wavered, then suddenly came back into focus.

I now found myself standing on the grass. The ground in front of me rippled and then seemed to unzip, the edges pulling apart like the two halves of a zipper, to show me stone steps leading down into the depths. Light glimmered up from out of the hole. It had a bluish tinge and silvery threadlike lines seemed to run through it, and lit the steps so I could see them clearly, and it was as if a line of light travelled down the middle of them showing the path and inviting me to step onto it. The darkness below called as well, it wanted me to go down there, then the light on the steps shivered slightly, rippling like water flowing over rocks, adding its summons.

I took a deep breath and set my foot onto the first step. The step stayed solid, taking my weight, so I brought the other foot down beside it. In this fashion, one foot at a time, I went slowly down the steps into the Earth and the light came with me, brightening, showing me more of the way. Some part of my brain was back with Alice and half expected to pass shelves with marmalade pots as she did when she fell down the rabbit hole, but this wasn't a rabbit burrow and I hadn't fallen into it but chosen of my own accord to walk down.

Down and down it went, deep into the Earth. At first I seemed to be passing soil but it soon turned into a rock tunnel and then at last, when I could no longer see the patch of sky above me, the steps stopped in front of a low archway. The slivery-blue light continued through the arch into a wider space, ducking down I followed to find myself in a cave.

It was like a room, furnished with table and chairs, shelves of bottles and books lined the opposite wall either side of a narrow dark opening, like a doorway. The light crossed the room to hover over a low bed and there he was, Merlin, but not as I'd ever seen him before. He seemed much older, like a man in his fifties with a short, neat beard, almost a caricature of the Merlin I'd known, like someone from a film. Then his eyes opened, full of laughter, and he chuckled. 'I borrowed it from your mind,' he said. 'Yes, it's a film, a very old one, you remember Excalibur with Nicol Williamson as me?'

Of course I did and this Merlin was very like Williamson's character, even dressed similarly, but minus the silver head cap. He'd got the voice right though and it made me laugh. 'So, what am I doing here then?' I asked.

'You've been looking at maps and saw the name, decided to come looking. And so you should after all these years! You want to see my crystal cave, don't you?' I nodded. 'Well here we are. This is sometimes where I live, where I sleep, where I wait ... until somebody comes looking for me.'

'I thought you were supposed to be sleeping in the cave until the time comes to rise up and help the world again. That's what it says in the stories,' I quizzed him.

He rolled his eyes and sat up. 'Ha! All very well but far too simplistic, and you know it. Indeed, I am waiting to help, but I help anyone who comes seriously looking for me.'

'Yes but this hill has been called Mynydd Myrddin for ages, hundreds of years at least.'

'Thousands,' he interrupted me. 'I've been lurking in this hill for aeons.'

'OK, but what am I doing here?'

He stood up and came over to the table, sat down and pointed to a chair opposite for me to take. 'What made you want to come here?' he asked.

I sat and thought for a bit. We hadn't long been in the house and I was learning about the land I'd come to live in, studying maps and reading stories, getting a feel for the old kingdom and found Mynydd Myrddin, then I'd seen that Caitlin Matthews, an old friend, knew it too. It all felt very 'meant'.

'It's about learning where I am and what it is you all want me to be doing here,' I said.

He grinned at that. 'Good,' he said. 'And so a visit to my

crystal cave is quite in order.' He sat watching me. There was something I wasn't doing, hadn't grasped, I could feel it. I looked around the room and my eye was pulled again to the dark opening in the wall. 'Aha!' he said. 'Good, you've noticed.'

The opening was narrow, more like a crevice in the rocks than a doorway, looking at it made the hairs on my neck stand up. 'So there's this cave, where you live ... and then there's a deeper cave, through there, where you ...?' I let the sentence trail off.

'So there is,' he nodded. 'And do you want to see what's down there?'

My skin crawled. I did ... and I didn't. A strong part of me wanted to rush back through the archway and flee back up the stairs, and I'd no idea why. Why should that opening scare me? I wasn't afraid of the dark and I'd been in lots of weird places before. 'What's through there?' I whispered.

'What are you most afraid of?'

Arrrrrgh! No! I didn't want to do that! Why didn't he make a cup of tea, do something simple and ordinary and normal like he usually did? 'I don't think I know,' I managed at last.

'Yes you do, even if you can't name it. And you know you do too.' His voice was more gentle now. 'What is it that scares you most? What do you think scares most people?'

My nails were clawing at the wooden table top, scratching rhythmically while my brain refused to operate. Breathing was difficult too, my chest felt tight. 'Power,' I whispered eventually. 'The power to be able to do things. If we have that, we've no excuse not to do it.'

'Precisely.' He paused. 'And are you going to wriggle any more or are you going to get up, come with me and look, go and get it?'

There was only one answer, of course, I had to go. He came round the table and took me by the hand. 'Come on, you can do this,' he told me softly. I followed him and we entered the dark opening. I could still see a bit from the light behind me and it really was a tunnel in the rock, narrow and vertical, with only just room for me to squeeze through. We soon left the light from the room behind us and were walking into complete darkness. I was feeling the wall with my free hand as I walked and very glad he was holding the other hand. It seemed to go on forever.

Suddenly the wall under my hand disappeared. I stopped and nearly lost my grip of Merlin's hand as he went on. He stopped. I could hear my breath rasping in my throat from fear. After a moment he tugged at my hand and I stepped forward again. I could see nothing at all, it was incredibly weird, I had no idea what would happen as I put each foot down, each step was pure blind faith that Merlin wouldn't lead me somewhere bad. As I realised this there was a change in the darkness, not light precisely but a sense of less dark. I kept on walking and I found I was breathing easier, I even felt a bit annoyed that I couldn't see, I wanted to see what was around me. I actually felt excited.

And there was less darkness again, in fact you could almost call it light now, just a glimmer but definitely light. I began to see walls around me, huge walls reaching far up to a domed ceiling, and they shone, twinkled almost like stars.

Then Merlin stopped. 'Got a bit of climb here,' he said, 'but there's steps. You'll manage. But we have to let go of each other as we need both hands to get up.' And he dropped my hand, just like that, and began to make his way upward. I could see better now, there were indeed steps, big and uneven, some of them even slanted, I was certainly going to need both hands. I got my foot on the first step and reached up for the next one to hang onto while I pulled myself up. Merlin was better at it than me – more practise obviously – so I was several steps behind him. At the top I found him sat on a ledge, he gave me a hand for the last pull up and I sat perched beside him, looking round.

I could see now, there was much more light, multi-coloured light, all blues and pinks and greens and yellows. I stared, and then I got it. The walls were covered in crystals. He began to chuckle, reading my mind, 'Well it *is* called the crystal cave,' he said. That made me laugh. 'I wanted to see your crystal cave and now I am,' I told him. 'So you are,' he said. 'And what's that doing for you?'

I sat for a while admiring the crystals while I thought about it. 'I didn't think I wanted to live at this house, in this place, did I? Not until everything else I wanted crashed and disappeared and this was all that was left. But you wanted me here and you weren't going to tell me that until I'd made the decision for myself and moved in. That's when the book fell on my head and I realised this is one of your places. So what am I to do here?'

'What is it you've always wanted to do but never have got around to doing, not properly?'

'Write,' I answered, quick as a flash. 'And so …' I was thinking out loud really, 'I've now got around to it. I'm here and you want me to write.'

'You were always asking for the space and time to write, weren't you? Well, here it is.' Then he chuckled again. 'Round tooits are always in such short supply you can never find one …'

'… but you, being a magician, managed to lay your hands on one for me!' I finished for him, grabbing his hand and squeezing it. 'Thank you, thank you so much.' I sat for a moment, full of the joy of getting what I wanted for, perhaps, the first time in my life. He squeezed my hand back.

'Well,' he replied, 'now you have it, you have to do it. You realise that, don't you?' I did indeed.

We clambered down the steps again and made our way back to his living-cave. It didn't seem to take nearly so long this time. Back at the table he now offered me tea, we sat sipping it. 'Yes, I'll write. I want to and there's a book raring to go. Will it work?' I finished nervously.

'Only if *you* work,' he retorted.

I went back through the arch and up the steps, out into the dip on the top of Merlin's Mountain. As I stepped back onto the grass

I saw the two halves of the ground zip themselves back up so there was no sign of the opening I'd gone through. And then I woke up, opened my eyes and found myself sitting looking at the long dragon's back of Hay Bluff.

I went home and began to write ... and I haven't stopped yet! I'm not likely to be stopping anytime until I'm dead.

6

Merlin and Broceliande

The Breton stories place Merlin in the ancient forest of Broceliande.

If you go to France, to Brittany, and travel about 18 miles west of Rennes, you find yourself at the forest of Paimpont, all that remains of the vast forest of Broceliande that once covered ancient inland Brittany.

The land is also known as Argoat, and Argoat was another uncanny Merlin connection for me that happened at school. I enjoyed French and learned to speak it very well, although I'm extremely rusty now, and this was largely through the agency of the young lady, Jeanne, we had to help us with spoken French. She was a university student who came over on a placement to spend a year at our school and she was very good. One of her suggestions I remember best was how to pronounce 'un petit', we were all getting it wrong, sounding like clumsy English folk on holiday, so she said, 'Non! You say it like the nursery rhyme, Umptey Dumpty, yes? Umptey, umptey, umptey!' I never forgot! But back to Merlin, she told us she came from Argoat, the old forested land that had been Broceliande, and showed us on the map where her parents lived.

Jeanne was about five years older than me but we became friends, she would visit with me at home on weekends and in the holidays when we would talk endlessly about Merlin and, indeed, we journeyed together to meet him.

This was not like journeying as per core shamanism. Back in those days, 1964, Michael Harner hadn't written his first book, and Mircea Eliade's first work was only just out and certainly hadn't been read by most of our folk although I think Dad did. The word shaman was known only in anthropological circles and the industry that now surrounds shamanism didn't exist. No, our journeys were what people might call daydreams, for dreaming is how my folk work. It's far closer to what Jung calls 'active imagination'. We would go off onto a hilltop, into the woods or by a stream or river and sit quiet and dream ...

Dreaming and imagination have been so degraded in the past 30-odd years, many people now seem to consider it a completely illusory process ... we have lost so much reality! It's the way I use and teach and it works, just as it did back in 1964, to transport you across and between the worlds. My French friend and I used it and had many encounters with Merlin, for she too came from a family of old ones in Brittany and her background was similar to mine.

Journey to Broceliande

One time that I especially recall was when we crossed to the Broceliande she knew and grew up in. We began our journey from a wild, empty hilltop a couple of miles from the village. We'd walked up there from home and brought a picnic. The sun was shining and it was hot; after we'd eaten we lay back against a big rock and closed our eyes, luxuriating in the warmth.

'This is like home,' Jeanne said. 'There's a hill like this that I go to and sometimes it takes me into the old forest. Shall we go there now?' Needless to say I agreed at once.

We were sat with our shoulders touching each other as well as the rock. Jeanne began to hum softly, a little wordless tune of mouth-music, repetitive and simple. It's a way my people use too, I began humming with her. The sound of the humming grew and grew, louder and louder in our ears but it wasn't us who were making the sound, it came from beyond us, outside us. We began to see ... see with our eyes still shut ... see another hilltop different and yet similar to the one we had walked to. And we were both seeing the same thing. We discussed it after when we came back, we were journeying together, the physical touch of our shoulders helped this to happen.

The hilltop in our dream was wilder than the one near my home, there was rough grass and heather as well as great stands of bracken and the rough grass was full of wildflowers. This was Jeanne's hill near her home in Brittany. A path led down the hill through the flowers and, in our journey, we got up and followed it. It took us down the hill and went into the forest. The forest edge was full of hazel and flowering trees, it felt as though we had come in late spring, perhaps April or May instead of the July we were in back at home. The scent of May-blossom filled the air. We entered the forest and were immediately surrounded by green-gold light as the sun filtered down through the bright, new, freshly-opened leaves.

We followed the path and soon heard the chuckling of a stream and in another few paces there it was, laughing and gurgling and splashing over the stones, and sometimes making that strange 'glooomph' noise as it dived between two bigger rocks. That's a sound I know so well from my home-river up on Exmoor. The stream flowed along beside our path as we continued, sometimes it leapt and fell over step-like falls, at others it ran deep below the path in clefts in the rock. It was now our leader, taking us to where we were meant to be. The path narrowed and the rocks rose up to either side, ferns hung down from them and the tree branches met overhead, we were in a green tunnel.

Rounding a rock, we found ourselves in a clearing. Tall, stately trees stood up around the edge and across from us two very ancient trees had grown together to form an arching doorway. They were covered in moss and their roots seemed to have risen out of the earth.

We sat down facing the tree arch and again the humming began. We weren't singing at all this time, the sound seemed to come from the trees themselves, then we saw movement and a figure materialised in the tree arch, stepped through and came towards us. The man's face was long, black hair hung to his shoulders and his eyes were very deep and dark; he was dressed in earth-coloured baggy trousers tucked into tall boots with a dark tunic over his shirt; on his belt hung a serviceable knife and a small axe.

'Hello,' he said, 'I'm glad you've come.' He folded himself up to sit cross-legged on the grass in front of us. 'You know me?'

Of course we did. 'Merlin,' I said. He laughed and nodded. 'You're doing well with the travelling.' (He often called journeying *travelling* with me). 'You've made it across the water now into another of my lands. What would you like to see today, now that you're here?'

'The fountains!' I blurted out immediately. Jeanne chuckled beside me.

'Yes,' she added, 'I'd like that too.'

'Which fountain do you want to see first ... most?'

'La Fontaine de Barenton,' Jeanne got in ahead of me.

Merlin chuckled. 'I suppose you want to try pouring water on the stone,' he said. We both blushed and grinned, of course we did! If you pour water from the spring over the stone at the fountain of Barenton then lightning flashes, thunder rolls, torrential rain strips the leaves from the trees and you find yourself in the middle of an adventure ... that's how the story tells it. Of course we wanted to try it.

He rose, all in one fluid motion like a snake. 'Come on then,' and he turned to the tree-arch. I was suddenly scared and Jeanne caught my arm. 'Afraid?' Merlin turned to us. 'You know how to go through a portal, don't you?' We did, of course, but this one was different, its energy was huge. I swallowed hard, took Jeanne's hand and pulled her to the archway, Merlin was already through it and stood watching us from the other side. Still holding hands, we each put our other hand on the trees to either side. It was like an electric shock going through us and suddenly we were through, without any conscious stepping forward.

'Phew!' I whispered. Merlin chuckled again.

He led us along a rocky path between great walls of stone, bigger and darker than the green tunnel we had come through earlier to get to the clearing. There was no sound now except the scrunching of our footsteps. It felt as if we'd been walking forever when suddenly Merlin stopped and we nearly ran into the back of him. We were at the edge of another clearing, but this one was darker and felt as if it was brooding.

In the centre was a mass of stone. We crossed towards it and saw it was what appeared to be a large cyst, a stone-lined chamber buried in the ground. A stone path led down into it between rock walls. It had obviously been built. We followed Merlin and stood beside him looking down into the stone chamber. There, at the bottom, we saw the glint of water. The water grew forming first a puddle and then a pool. In the back of the cyst-like structure we now noticed a piece of white rock crystal sticking out of the wall and, below it, a small niche which contained a metal bowl. Just like in the stories. Now, which of us was going to take the bowl, fill it with water and pour it over the stone?

'Be careful what you wish for,' Merlin said softly, startling us, 'for you will certainly get it.' We'd actually forgotten he was there in the excitement of seeing the stories come to life. 'Come and sit down over here,' he told us, so we did.

He took out his water flask and offered it to us. I took it and was just about to drink when I remembered. 'What happens if I drink this?' I asked him. 'That's better! Getting your wits back now are you?' He took the flask back from me and took a swig himself. 'There! There's nothing now that will change or harm you,' he said and passed it back to me.

I took it, held it in both hands and asked for myself, 'Is it appropriate for me to drink from this flask?' I got a yes, so I drank, it was cold, clear water, very refreshing. I passed it to Jeanne and she did the same, asking for herself. Merlin was smiling now, pleased with us.

'Mmmm! Better,' Merlin said. 'You two had lost your wits on that walk, off with the fairies you were, you'd better take your shirts off and put them on backwards to make sure.' That's an old remedy that usually works; you take your jacket or shirt off and put it on again inside-out. It brings your consciousness back from la-la-land. 'Now … what was it in the way of adventure you were wanting?' he asked us once we had our shirts on inside-out.

'I think …' Jeanne began, 'we were off with the fairies right from the beginning today.'

'So do I,' I said. 'We wanted out of the everyday world, we wanted the romance of the old stories, to adventure, to play.'

'Well you got that didn't you? You made it over here to Brittany, to Broceliande.'

'And we met you,' I added. 'But somehow that wasn't enough, we wanted more. And the Barenton fountain is always so exciting in the stories.'

'You're neither of you children any more. What is travelling all about?' We both thought for a moment. 'About learning?' Jeanne said.

'It certainly is!' he agreed. 'So what have you learned today?' That made us both blush.

'Not be childish and want adventure just for the fun of it,' I said.

'Yes,' he agreed. He stood up and went to the fountain, took the metal bowl and filled it. 'So what would you be asking if I were to pour the water over the stone?'

We sat thinking, what would we want? Did we really want all the knights and horses, silk dresses and troubadour romance? Yes, part of us did, I was 16 and Jeanne just 21, both of us well young enough to want Hollywood-style romantic dreams. But was that really what we wanted? We were both bright enough to know that those dreams would be no more meaningful than going to see a film; we didn't really want to live our lives in that sort of pink-n-fluffy way.

'To know our feet are on the right path,' I said into the silence. Jeanne nodded.

Merlin poured the water over the white rock crystal. Lightning didn't flash nor thunder roll, the poor trees were not stripped of their leaves by hailstones. At first we thought nothing at all had happened and then we saw it. Across from us, seeming to go out from the source of the spring, was a path. Sunlight shone down on it, the trees above it had parted to allow the light through and there, in the middle of the green stood a robin. He chirped to us.

'Ooooooo!' we both breathed. This was far more impressive than knights and palfreys and silken dresses!

'He's waiting for you,' Merlin told us softly.

We stood up, looked at Merlin and our eyes met his. 'Thank you,' we whispered. Then we set off down the path, the robin chirruped again and flew on before us.

We awoke softly as the sun was sinking low down in the sky and the shadow of the rock had grown very long on the wild hilltop near my home. We smiled to each other, but there was nothing to say. We packed up our picnic and walked the two miles back home in the summer gloaming. We had had our adventure and it was far, far more than the story ideas we'd talked about as we'd walked out to the hill in the morning. It was a very good day.

The Fontaine de Barenton

The Fontaine de Barenton in the Forest of Broceliande, where we went in our journey, has long been associated with Merlin. Its waters are known for their therapeutic virtues, one of which is to treat madness, and that brings us again to Merlin as wild man of the woods. Nearby the fountain is the hamlet of Folle Pensée (which means crazy thought). It grew up in the 12th century and was named from the Old French words Fol Pansi, which means to heal insanity. When Jeanne and I arrived at the fountain we were, as Merlin said, off with the fairies, into crazy romantic dreams. Sitting by the fountain with him brought us back to sanity and reality.

In Brittany they say the fountain is dedicated to the worship of Belenos, our old All-Father god Beli, the father of Lludd and Llefellys. He's a sun god, fire and light. They think it's possible the name of the fountain, Barenton, might be a contraction of Belenos, perhaps through Balanton, then Belenton, until it finally became Barenton. Whatever, it certainly has a strong effect on those whose wits have gone a-wool-gathering.

The fountain is also associated with Vivien, and it's said that Merlin stood on the stone slab by the spring to initiate Vivian to the magical rituals. The stone is called the Perron (meaning stone) de Belanton or Perron de Merlin.

The fountain is also linked to the story of Ywain, Knight of the Lion, whose tale is told in a romance by Chrétien de Troyes; it's also associated with the romance of Lancelot as the Knight of the Cart and Chrétien's romance includes several references to the Lancelot poem. These stories are the ones that say if the fountain's water is poured over the stone, the perron, then a storm comes that rips the leaves off the trees, followed by the appearance of a Black Knight who challenges whoever has poured the water. It's an initiation story that offers you the opportunity to cross the threshold into the scary unknown and there find your way through the challenges that will come.

The fountain and its stone together are a gateway between worlds, and both Vivien and Merlin are its threshold keepers, the liminal guardians who enable those who wish to cross over and walk between worlds. As in the journey Jeanne and I took, Merlin tricks and teases you, questions you, tries to awaken you so you're aware of just precisely what you're asking. The challenges that each of us gets this way, by pondering and asking, are far greater than having to fight with Black Knights!

The legends survived the Christian invasion and during the Middle Ages the villagers were still invoking rain in times of drought by dipping a cross in its water. In the 19th century the place was 'restored' and integrated into Christian celebrations. The last Christian procession to the well happened in 1925, but modern visitors hold their own celebrations as a mark of respect for both the well and for Merlin. The pagan beliefs have never died, but only lain hidden and buried deep under the Christian rites. We have our ways of keeping the stories alive, and reverence along with asking at the fountain continues to this day.

Wildmen and Woods

The earliest known written stuff on Merlin is as the woodsman, the man who lives in the woods, the wildman of the woods. It goes far, far deeper than the relatively well known (and quite recent in human history terms) story of the Battle of Arderydd of AD 573, which says he ran into the woods because he was so shocked at the deaths of the battle. I have serious doubts about this as a reason for Merlin doing anything, it's a very human reason ... and we must remember that Merlin is *not* a human, but an otherworldly being. He doesn't feel as we might about death, or anything else.

Forests are an integral part of our stories and the woods have been part of our mythos and heritage for as long as we've lived in Britain – a mythos is a story or set of stories that are significant for a particular culture or society. Current archaeological finds show that people have lived in Britain for the best part of a million years at least, and future finds may perhaps show us to have been here much longer. Back in those long-gone days when we weren't living by the seashore we lived in the woods. Woods covered just about all of the temperate parts of Planet Earth until maybe 10,000 years ago when we began cutting them down to make fields. Even after this trees, groves and glades were special sacred spaces for us; the great old ones, the goddesses and the gods, held them as their nemetons and they still do.

The word nemeton is linked to the Nemetes tribe who lived by the Rhine between the Palatinate and Lake Constance in what is now Germany. They held woods and glades sacred to their goddess Nemetona, so the word has now come to mean a sacred space. Inscriptions and place-names related to the word nemeton occur all across the Celtic world.

But we have been left a very limited idea of what these groves are about, or we have if we rely only on written records. Those come largely from the Romans and this example from Lucan's Pharsalia, describing a grove near Massilia, shows you just how biased these reports can be. (Massilia is the town we now know as Marseilles.) We have to remember that Lucan's point of view is very different to that of the local people he's describing. He thought of them as savages, and his description really does do its best to evoke a shiver of delicious horror up the spines of his Roman audience:

> ... *no bird nested in the nemeton, nor did any animal lurk nearby; the leaves constantly shivered though no breeze stirred. Altars stood in its midst, and the images of the gods. Every tree was stained with sacrificial blood. The very earth groaned, dead yews revived; unconsumed trees were surrounded with flame, and huge serpents twined round the oaks. The people feared to approach the grove, and even the priest would not walk there at midday or midnight lest he should then meet its divine guardian.*

Lucan's lurid description suggests he thought of us all as 'nasty, brutish and short' to misquote Thomas Hobbes' memorable description of life outside his own modern society. That view still persists today. It's not only utterly wrong but seriously inhibits understanding our ancestors. Lucan and the other Roman writers are very much suspect. Like all journalists, they had to appeal to their audience who, in this case, needed to believe that the conquered folk were rubbish compared to themselves. For me, the Roman writers are the Rupert Murdochs of their day and about as trustworthy for giving you the real story.

For us woods are beautiful and sacred places, they're thresholds, especially the entering of them. One of the ways we've always used as an initiation is to send the initiate off into the woods alone, and they must find their own way in, not use a path already made by others before them. They will know they are on the right path because, somehow, the way they carve for themselves will not be *too* hard for them; it will be incredibly hard, but not too hard. If they try to enter where another has gone before then their path, which maybe looked easy at first, will be strewn with obstacles and dangers. This is beautifully illustrated in Thomas of Erceldoune's song, Thomas the Rhymer:

O see not ye yon narrow road,
So thick beset wi thorns and briers?
That is the path of righteousness,
Tho after it but few enquires.
And see not ye that braid braid road,
That lies across yon lillie leven?
That is the path of wickedness,
Tho some call it the road to heaven.

The song is a bit Christianised. The words righteousness and wickedness are not concepts we use in the old ways as they're too simplistic – but otherwise it says it right for the initiation process. You go looking for the way that appears beset with thorns and briars rather than the broad road across the lily fields.

Merlin's woods are like this and his own journey too. He feels the call, and flees into the woods to make his home there with the wild creatures of the wood. He doesn't choose the easy path, but his path becomes a way of life, he is the Wildman of the Woods. He lives with a pig as a familiar spirit, it's also one of the totems of our goddess Ceridwen, and with an apple tree, which is a symbol for the Apple Woman. Ceridwen is the lady of the cauldrons, she is maiden, mother and crone all at the same time, goddess of rebirth, transformation, and inspiration. She is both creation and destruction, and all the life in between those two. The Apple Woman is a goddess of death, and of thresholds. In one of the stories she poisons Merlin with apples set out beneath the tree, but her apples give wisdom that also invokes madness by setting the world upside-down. Apples have this quality of giving wisdom at high cost through many traditions, even the peoples of the Book use them in their mythos of Adam and Eve and, there again, it is the feminine who gives that wisdom to the masculine – the goddess educates the god, leading him out of old ways and into new. The meaning of the word educate comes from the Latin *educare* which means 'to lead out', so the goddess leads out the god. The apples hark to Thomas the Rhymer too, for the fairy queen stops Thomas taking the fruit too soon, before he is ready for it; she is teaching him and leading him out, and Thomas has a huge connection with Merlin.

We've talked about Myrddin Wyllt, the Wildman, so let's now look at Merlin as Custennin, the giant herdsman. Custennin has some of his old places close by where I now live in the Welsh Marches, so not only do I live in one of the places where Merlin was born, but I also live in a place where he was Custennin too.

In some of the stories, Custennin is said to be the son of the Elen who wed with Macsen Wledig – she is one of the forms/incarnations of our Elen of the Ways – although he wasn't a son of Macsen as far as the stories say. He's a central figure in the story of Culhwch and Olwen, which comes from the *Red Book of Hergest* and there's also a fragmented version of it in the *White Book of Rhydderch*, and it's the longest of the surviving Welsh prose tales. In the story, Culhwch and his companions find Custennin sat on top of a tump carrying a great club and surrounded by every sort of animal. He helps them by telling them where to find Olwen, explaining his relationship to her and her father, and telling them how to go on so Culhwch can win her as his bride.

Culhwch and Olwen is a whole lot more than a simple folktale. It's steeped in lore and tells how the old king must be replaced by the young one who, in his turn, will become the old king and be replaced himself ... it's the story of the cycle of life-death-rebirth.

Custennin, the Lord of the Forest and Lord of the Animals, the herdsman who cares for all the beasts, and all the plants too, is a deep principle of our tradition and Merlin uses this guise to show us what it means. The herdsman is the husbandman of the goddess. He is her guardian, he takes care of her in all her forms and in all places while she, of course, is the land, the Earth and the container for all of life.

Merlin is the Woodwose too. The word comes from the Anglo-Saxon *Wuduwasa*, which means man-of-the-woods, a man-like creature whose body is covered with thick hair and who is found in the folktales throughout Europe. Like Custennin, he often carries a big club and is found in the woods surrounded with the animals. Interestingly, the British family name Woodhouse likely comes from this.

One of my favourite poets, Ted Hughes, wrote a whole series of poems under the title of *The Wodwo*, and they are amongst my favourite poems. In Britain, Hughes casts a long and very wonderful shadow over 20th century poetry, from 1957 to his death in 1998. In an era that saw poetry virtually dissolve into formlessness, Hughes' poetry is squarely anchored in the heart of metaphysics, mysticism, and ancient British mythology..

In the mythology of the British Isles and Europe, the Woodwose is a link between the forest creatures, such as elves and nymphs, and humans; he stands between them and us as intermediary, and this one of Merlin's threshold functions. Close analogies to him might be the better known figures Puck and

Pan. The wild woodsman is a deep, ancient, and vital spirit in Europe and across the world, it's a necessary link back to our primal connection between the natural world and the spirit world. The wild man's companion is the goddess of the land. Together they are the yin and yang, feminine and masculine, the lady and lord as we call them. To lose the link with the wild man is to lose the fundamental connection to spirit. If we lose this we lose our knowing, kenning, of who we are, and our connection to the goddess, the Earth herself.

In Ted Hughes' poem the Wodwo does not yet know who, what or where he is – he asks, 'What am I?' at the beginning of the poem. He goes on to ask, 'What am I? What is my name? What does the forest call me? Do I have an owner?' He feels that he is of the world but not anchored to it. Hughes takes us right into the mind of the wildman himself as he snuffles around the side of a stream, looking for who he is and how he links with everything around him. Hughes talks, too, about the threads, the spirit-mycorrhiza, that connect us to everything.

I've no threads
fastening me to anything I can go anywhere
I seem to have been given the freedom
of this place what am I then?

Hughes experiences the Wodwo himself in the poem, as he writes it, as do each of us who read it, and he finds his context within the landscape. The Wodwo searches for consciousness and in so doing defines the nature of consciousness itself, for himself. Hughes' skill as a poet enables us to know the Wodwo is inside ourselves. This is part of what the shaman does, and Hughes is a shaman as he offers us a gateway through his poetry, through which we can see and, if we dare, go through and so come to 'know everything'. The shaman is liminal, he or she is a threshold, just as Merlin is.

7

Vivien: Keeper of Doorways

Many of us know the stories of Merlin and his lover. She's most commonly known as Vivien or Nimue. My parents named me for her, as Vivien, and although I don't use the name except in private I feel myself as deeply in contact with her as I do with Merlin.

The Vivien stories have become the kernels for novels, films and TV series. Most of them show her as his enemy, the one who betrays him and eventually locks him up inside a hawthorn tree, or a cave, or a rock. But not all the old stories say this, the Breton stories are very different and show Vivien as Merlin's lover and soul-mate, partner and confidante.

Vivien is a fascinating character and a spirit whose nature is very much hidden in plain sight. Just about anyone who's heard of Merlin has also heard of her, but what most people know of her is usually wrong. She's very hard to know, she hides herself in shadow.

Brittany, particularly Armorica and the forest of Paimpont, that last remaining bit of Broceliande is, perhaps, the place with the most stories about her. There, they tell that Vivien's father was a human man called Dyonas whose patron was Diana, the deer-goddess and huntress. The stories of that time (circa 1230/40, by Sir Thomas Malory) give us hints and clues only. There are grains of truth through them, but you need to 'quest' your way through them because Malory wrote for his audience and so, as ever, the foot gets cut to fit the shoe. To those who know the old ways, the story suggests that the otherworldly goddess, Diana, seduced Dyonas in order to become pregnant with Vivien.

Vivien having a human father and an otherworldly mother is

the grain of truth. We're back with the magical child again, but this time the other way up to Merlin. And that makes sense too. He comes through a human mother and a spirit father and carries the masculine energy; she reverses that process coming through a spirit mother and a human father and carries the feminine energy. And that takes to another of the fundamentals of our tradition, the twining of *both* energies, the feminine and the masculine, is the way the magic is made. Not *either/or* but *and/and* ... two sides of one coin. Inclusive and integrating, not exclusive and separative.

You can likely see how these attitudes would be uncomfortable if not downright subversive to the early Norman lords! For them the male is the ruler, women are property, chattels. The only overall power they allow is their god, and he is masculine! The real Merlin and Vivien would upset this applecart and breed disruption of their rule. So we have been left with stories that contain little grains of truth smothered in great swathes of propaganda that support the Norman status quo. That makes realising the truth hard. Add in the Roman stories of how we lived – e.g. Lucan's description of the sacred grove – and you understand what a mish-mash we've been left with. But it is all still here for us to know, we just have to go questing, searching, divining and discerning ... but that's what the awenydd does anyway!

Merlin and Vivien are the coming together of the two energies that we'll call the feminine and the masculine. We could just as easily call them negative/positive as in electricity, or yin/yang, or receptive/creative as in the Tao, or inner/outer, or grail/spear to come back to the Arthurian stories again. That is what the grail/spear imagery in our stories is about, the working together of the twin energies that we know best as feminine and masculine, lady and lord, goddess and god.

Merlin holds the masculine energies through his spirit-father and human-mother while his lady, Vivien, holds the feminine energies through her spirit-mother and human-father. Their relationship reminds me of this picture of the yin-yang ... she is Moon to his Sun.

It's a very alchemical symbol. To borrow from this much more modern tradition, if we look into alchemical practices we see that the old alchemists often worked in pairs, the feminine and the masculine, the sister and brother or sacre souria and sacre frère. In this way they were able to combine energies really well and the concept goes right back to our own old ways where the god is guardian to the goddess. This is how Merlin and Vivien work.

Lady of the Lake

The Château de Comper is three kilometres east of the little village of Concoret in the département of Morbihan, right in the old forest of Broceliande. It's now a centre for the Merlin and Vivien stories, which have continued to grow over the past couple of thousand years. The castle is gloriously turreted, straight out of a Disney film set – the French and Germans do fairy-tale castles so very well – and it now houses the Centre de l'Imaginaire Arthurien. Going there somewhat reminds me of going to the Arthurian Hall in Tintagel; it too does exhibitions, events and themed walks!

If you can drag yourself away from these delights then behind the Chateau de Comper you'll find a large lake. It's here that Merlin is said to have built his crystal tower, deep under the water, and he built it for Vivien. Find a quiet spot to sit and contemplate and you may find yourself on a journey beneath the waters to visit the crystal tower. The old Bretton stories call Vivien a 'lady of the lake'; this is her particular pond.

This story of Merlin building the crystal tower for Vivien is a lot different to the usual story that she locks Merlin up there and runs off with all his magic. Seeing her as thief and wicked woman has never felt right to me. In my experience with them both, she's always been his co-worker, the other half of Merlin, Moon to his Sun. He's never appeared as some half-witted old man who would be deceived by a lovely young woman, far from it. And Vivien herself has never seemed to be a deceiver either, but a strong lady who knows what she's about and both wishes and needs to work with the masculine, with Merlin. The vibrant duality of the two of them makes sense in our old ways, the masculine and feminine are not in conflict, but two halves of one whole.

The crystal tower in the lake is also a star-gazing tower. It's the place of 70 doors and 70 windows where they worked together and with the cosmos.

Doors and the Valley of No-Return

Another place in Broceliande that is associated with Merlin is Tréhorenteuc, La Porte du Dedans, which means the Door of the Within. The name says so much, the doorway inside one's self, the doorway we all go through time and time again, the threshold that we cross every time we expand our consciousness and open ourselves to new things. We all need to open our door within, and to cross over its threshold, indeed to do this many times. It's yet another lesson that Merlin and Vivien teach us.

A stone's throw from La Porte du Dedans is the Val-Sans-Retour, the Valley of No Return. It's a shady valley cut in the red schist-stone of the region, a strange, wild and beautiful place, or so it was when I was last there 30-odd years ago.

The name, Valley of No Return, conjures up all sorts of things but, for me, they're not terrifying or threatening. It's all about thresholds, yet again. When you cross a threshold, go from here to there, there's no way you can come back to the same place you left, it's just not possible. The time is different now, and the place will have changed in that time. You cannot return to who and what you were, nor to the time you were, for it will all be gone, different.

Ursula K Le Guin puts this beautifully in her 1974 book *The Dispossessed* where says, '*You can always go home as long as you realise home is a place you have never yet been.*'

We can never go back ... we can never return, yesterday is always gone and tomorrow hasn't yet come, the only time we can live in is now. Even in time-travel the yesterday or tomorrow we might visit is not the one that is happening now.

From an even earlier time this 1970 song by Mike Heron of The Incredible String Band sings it perfectly too ...

This Moment

This moment is different from any before it, this moment is different,
  it is now.
And if I don't kiss you that kiss is untasted I'll never, no never, get
  it back
But why should I want to, I'll be in the next moment,
Sweet moment, sweet lover, sweet now.
The walls of this room are different from any before them,
They are now, they are now.
The air that you breathe is different from any before it,
It is now, it is now.
You may think that life is repeating,
Repeating, Repeating, Repeating, Repeating.
You may think that life is repeating,

Oh no, Oh no, Oh no, Oh no, Oh no!
Each moment is different from any before it,
Each moment is different, it's now.

Merlin is about this perpetual and eternal now. That's part of what being a threshold is about. It's hard for many of us to grasp though because we're so encouraged to believe time is linear. It is, in the basics of everyday life. You can organise yourself around a clock and a calendar and we all do so for everyday convenience … but what happens when you get off Earth, or when you travel near to, at (or even beyond) the speed of light? Then time is not the same, it flows differently. A day on Jupiter for instance is only about 10 hours long! That's because Jupiter spins, faster on its axis than any other planet. But a year on Jupiter is 12 times as long as a year on Earth because that's how long it takes for Jupiter to make one trip around the Sun.

When you begin to think of space-travel time gets very different to our simple linear version on Earth. We talk about the nearest star to us, Alpha Centauri, as being about four light-years away. Light travels at 186,000 miles per second. Take a deep breath and read that again! In the time it takes to say 'one-and' light has travelled 186,000 miles. If you like to either do the sums or look it up you'll find that in one earthly year (365 of our days) light travels nearly six million, million miles. So four light-years – the distance to Alpha Centauri – is roughly four times six million, million miles, or 24 million, million miles. That's big!

Likely your head is beginning to spin, let's spin it a bit more. The light that arrives at your eyeball from Alpha Centauri gives you pictures of what was happening there four years ago. Not now. You would be seeing Alpha Centauri in the past. If you took off in a space ship that could go as fast as light it would take you four of our-length years to get there and four to come back, so when you got home again everyone you knew would be eight years older.

But ... here comes the really mind boggling bit ... you would *not* be eight years older, you'd be almost the same age as when you started off, assuming you didn't stop over when you got there. That's because you would be all the time travelling at the speed of light and, as Einstein showed us, this means your time is different from those of your mates back on Earth, and it's also different to that of the folk on Alpha Centauri.

Phew! So time depends on what you're looking at and where you're looking from – a maxim Merlin gave me some 40-plus years ago. We, each of us, always, live in our own now. It's one we cannot return to, nor extend, and we see from the perspective of that now.

We can watch happenings in other times and places – we call this far-fetching, day-dreaming, far or remote viewing, travelling and journeying – but those times and places are not our now.

Shamanic peoples all around the world have always made their own concepts for this and they're often remarkably similar. One I like that comes from outside of my own old ways is that of the Navajo people. It's the same as ours – time is not linear but a spiral. So you return to Earth from your space-trip but that Earth is on a different arm of the spiral from where it was when you left.

As you work your way through the knowings, the kennings, you go from a simple linear idea of time to begin to think of it as a circle, through the ideas of cycles, seasons and rebirth.

Gradually you come to realise that this doesn't fully cover all the options either and you begin to explore the spiral. Then you begin to find this takes you a whole lot further and deeper into kenning the mysteries of life, the universe and everything.

As you work further you come to see breathing as part of this, breathing in, breathing out, but as the song says, '*The air that you breathe is different from any before it, It is now, it is now*'. And, as the song goes on to say, life is not repeating, it is continuously different, and that each moment is different from any before it, each moment is different, it is now. This is quite a leap. It means standing perpetually on the edge, and being content with this.

Merlin wants, and needs, us to get this, to know it in our bones, and if we ask him he will help us to do it.

Doorways

Dad and Mum first took me to Exmoor when I was hardly more than a baby. I remember staggering around on unsteady baby-legs at the edge of the Barle river, and falling in and being rescued, and thinking falling in was rather fun so going and doing it again!

Then Mum died of cancer when I was three-and-a-half so going with her didn't last long, but Dad continued to take me so I gradually got to know the two moors; Dartmoor where I was born and lived until I was about eight and Exmoor where we then came to live.

Soon after we came to live on the edge of Exmoor I got my first pony. She was a little Exmoor mare with the mealy-muzzle and a load of attitude, just thirteen-two hands high, and she became my soul-mate and familiar until I grew too tall to ride her any more. She was called Jewel and we used to spend every conceivable moment together, before and after school, weekends and all the holidays. We very often we rode out onto Exmoor, which was only about twelve miles as the crow flies ... or the pony trots ... and took us about one-and-a-half hours. We knew the farmers and, as long as we behaved properly with gates and didn't disturb cattle or sheep, we could ride across their fields and through the woods.

One of our favourite places to go was the woods along the Barle. The way we rode there took us up over the high moor and then down into the woods. When we arrived at the river we followed a path to a meadow-like place at the edge of the trees high above the river.

Just back in the trees was an old, somewhat dilapidated,

woodsman's hut that nobody seemed to use any more. Like the Exmoor trees, it was covered in ferns that hung all over the roof and clung to the timber walls, its cobweb-covered windows let in some greenish light and the door creaked delightfully on its hinges. Jewel and I would camp there of an evening and go back home the next day, or else go on exploring to another camp maybe up on the moor or down in Horner Woods. Life for children, especially country children, was very different back then in the 1950s and early 1960s. Parents didn't fuss as they do now, but made sure their children were up for all the adventures they wanted to do, like camping out, making fires, cooking food and boiling a kettle for tea, using a compass and a map, and knowing how to look after themselves. And I knew how to look after Jewel too. It was very like the descriptions in the story *Swallows and Amazons* from even longer ago in the 1920s, only with ponies instead of boats. I suspect lots of modern kids would be very jealous of us.

So Jewel and I would go off to the moor and stay out all night. Jewel would graze in the meadow while I camped in the hut. We had some wonderful adventures. You see it was more than just an old woodsman's hut, it was one of the places where I would meet with Merlin. As I've said, I've met him in lots of places all through all my life, and still do. By the time I was eight or nine, with my pony Jewel, I'd got a handle on working with him without letting other children know, unless they too had parents who were old ones, as my horsey-friend Roseanne did.

One time I particularly remember going up to the hut was of an evening in June when I was about twelve. The weather was lovely, all the trees had on their new summer dresses of translucent green, the meadow was full of flowers and it was the beginning of summer half-term so there was no need to get back. I'd finished my sausage and bacon supper and was sat in the doorway of the hut listening to the robin singing evensong and sipping my tin mug of tea (I still have that mug!) when there was a rustle behind me. I looked round to see a shadowy figure stood near the back wall beside a door ... where there certainly never had been a door before.

'Hello,' he said, 'any more tea in the pot?' Of course it was Merlin, looking rather like my Uncle Jack this time, with his corduroy trousers tucked into tall leather boots and a leather jerkin over his shirt, the dress of a woodsman. He came to sit in the doorway with me and produced a tin mug, apparently from nowhere, so I poured him some tea. 'I thought you might like to see somewhere else this evening,' he went on after a short while, 'through the door.' He cocked his head back towards the wall where the door had appeared.

'Where does it go?'

'Anywhere you like,' he grinned.

'Really?' I replied ironically.

'Yes, really.' He looked at me. 'Anywhere you wish.' He paused and sipped the tea. 'That's the thing,' he went on, 'it opens to anywhere you wish.'

Hmmm! I nodded, getting what he meant. 'So I have to wish very carefully ...' I was thinking of some places I'd rather not find myself, like back at school! Merlin nodded. 'Might I be able to go where you live?' I asked.

He laughed at that. 'I live everywhere ... what are you thinking of?'

'I was thinking about the old stories, like when you lived with the pig under the apple tree.'

'We could do that,' he replied, 'if you can hold the picture clearly in your head. Can you?' And with that he put the picture into my mind. It was clear and distinct, a wooden shelter not unlike where we sat, but with an apple tree in full blossom to the side, its branches dipping down over the roof and half covering the window. A young ginger pig snuffled in the grass around its roots. 'Got it?' I nodded, holding my breath.

We got up and went to the door. My hand tingled as I lifted

the latch. It opened and I stepped down onto the grass. At first I thought I hadn't gone anywhere, it looked very like the wood at the back of my own hut.

'Go on,' said Merlin, right behind me, nearly making me jump out of my skin, I'd forgotten he was there. 'Round the side. We've come out the back.'

Round the side of the hut I saw it was different. For a start, this one looked in better nick than mine, there were no ferns growing in the walls and no cobwebs on the window, and there was no meadow in front, and no Jewel either. 'She's fine,' Merlin had read my mind. 'She knows where we are, no need to fret. Come inside.'

He led the way up a couple of steps and I realised his hut was built on a platform above the ground, unlike mine, and it had a veranda too, which mine didn't. Much posher! Inside, it was a single room with a big stove in a chimney on the side wall, a table, bench and a large carver-chair, there was a bed in an alcove in the other side-wall. The back wall held a door just like the one I'd come through from my hut. Merlin pulled a big black kettle from the back of the stove onto the hob – the stove looked awfully like our Rayburn at home and he grinned at me as, again, he caught my thought. 'Borrowed from you mind,' he told me. 'And anyway it's more convenient, if less romantic, than cauldrons hanging on chains over an open fire.' I had to grin back, he'd told me before that magic is ultra-practical. 'Thought we might make another brew while you explore.'

I went round the hut, touching everything, it all felt quite solid and just like the furniture at home. I sat down on the bench by the table. He brought the tea over, with a couple of pottery mugs this time, and sat opposite me in the carver chair, it was very obviously his.

'Doors,' he began, 'what do you think about doors?'

Whenever Merlin asks me questions there's always a lot more to it than the obvious surface connotations. I thought about it as

I sipped the tea. 'You go from here to there,' I said.

'And what about from there to here?' he asked. 'Or don't you want to get back to your hut, and Jewel, again?'

I did, of course. 'So doors go both ways ...' I stopped. 'Does that mean past and future too?'

'Yes, both ways.'

'So time travel is possible ...?' I was thrilled.

'Ha!' he snorted, 'not so fast! It's that kind of thinking that could mess up everything. If you go forward or back in time you have to be utterly still or else you could change things ... you might change them so you no longer exist!' His eyebrows shot up and he looked really scary.

'Bu-but what's the point of the door then, if going through it might mess things up? Have I messed up by coming here, now?' I was really worried, what if I never saw Jewel again, or Dad, or my stepmother Vera?

'It's OK,' he smiled, 'you've not messed up. But I want you to see what doorways are about. Here isn't the same as there. Then isn't the same as now, whether it's future or past. Come and look at this.'

He got up and went to the ordinary door out onto the veranda. I followed him to the apple tree, it was old and gnarled with a great thick trunk. He was pointing at something carved into the bark, it was a spiral, well more than a spiral, it was a labyrinth. I followed the pattern with my finger, the way took me in and out around the paths and, eventually, after going almost into the middle and then back out all round the outer ring, I found myself at the centre. I traced the way back out again. Then I did it again.

'It goes in and it comes out,' I said. 'It leads you in and then it leads you out.' I felt I'd got hold of something, but I didn't know what it was. I let my finger run the pattern a third time.

'Yes,' he said slowly. 'It does.'

He stood there, watching me staring at the labyrinth. Slowly it began to come a little clearer.

'More tea?' He interrupted my thinking.

I followed him back inside and sat at the table with my finger still tracing the pattern on the top of the table. I could feel it, even if I couldn't see it, in the polished wood of the table.

'Doorways take you places, and they take you times too. The now you arrive at through the door isn't the same now you left when you opened it.'

'But they're both now ...' I added.

'Yes they are. And they both exist at the same time, although both the time and the place are different.'

'And the places are all there too, even if the times are different.' I felt I was getting somewhere, even if I hadn't a clue where! 'And ... and the doorway is sort of like the labyrinth. It leads you to the centre and it leads you out again. But the centre isn't the same each time you go there ...'

Merlin smiled. 'I think you're getting it,' he said. 'And you have to know where you are as well as where you're going so you can come back.'

'And that's what the labyrinth does?'

He nodded. 'It helps you know when and where you are.' We sat sipping tea, then he said, 'Time to go back to Jewel now, I think.'

I followed him through the back door of his hut, back through the back door of my own hut, and ran out of my front door and there was Jewel standing by it looking in to see if I was there. I hugged her neck and stroked her nose, it was very good to know she was still there for me.

'Time for bed too,' Merlin added. He turned to the back of my hut, went through the door ... and then there was no door in the back wall of my hut any more.

Jewel lay down in the grass by our hut. I grabbed my sleeping bag and curled up against her back. She was warm and solid, I slept well.

Not long after this Dad took me down to Cornwall. We drove

through the village of Boscastle and up over the hill to drop down into the head of Rocky Valley. He parked the car and we walked down through the woods to the ruins of the old Trewethit Mill, below where he used to live during WWII. He showed me the Bronze Age labyrinths carved into the rock wall behind the mill ... they were like the one carved into Merlin's apple tree.

I still visit them regularly and, always, going through their doorway takes me somewhere I've not been before, and then it brings me back again.

8

Merlin and Liminal Thresholds

Merlin is a god of *edges*. He is without limits.

He brings us to the brink of what we know and helps us leap off the cliff into what we don't yet know. He stands at crossings, borders and frontiers, places of initiation where we go from one state to another, and takes us to the rim of the world, the rim of our knowing, and then on and out beyond, he helps us move beyond our limits and climb out of the box we've been living in up to then.

Merlin is often called uncanny, meaning something that is strangely familiar as well as unknown. He is indeed enigmatic, shadowy, cryptic and covert. He, like the threshold, is both mysterious and also strangely familiar for, whether we remember or not, we really have been there before.

Once you get your head, and your everyday logic, out of the way you discover that actually it's not necessary to know Merlin completely, or indeed to know anything completely. We don't need ultimate answers to anything ... although we are often told we do. We modern folk are inculcated and constrained to believe we should be able to explain every single solitary thing. But we can't and we never do. This is a very modern complaint, even only a few hundred years ago we knew very well that there is so much that is unknowable. Hamlet's quotation to Horatio is perhaps one of the best known ways of saying this, *'There are more things in heaven and earth, Horatio, than are dreamt of in your philosophy.'* That, for me, gives a whacking big clue to our difficulties with the idea of answers ... our philosophies.

The unknowable is always out there, but it isn't impenetrable and science confirms this. We can and do know more as our consciousness expands to let it in, but there is always more to know. As Isaac Newton said, '*I do not know what I may appear to the world, but to myself I seem to have been only like a boy playing on the sea-shore, and diverting myself in now and then finding a smoother pebble or a prettier shell than ordinary, whilst the great ocean of truth lay all undiscovered before me.*' If that incredible natural philosopher and alchemist can say this, how can we all not also feel it in ourselves?

The really good research-science knows this too. I'm talking about places like CERN, the Rutherford-Appleton Laboratories, the Culham Science Centre near Abingdon, and the Laser Interferometer Gravitational-Wave Observatory (LIGO) in the USA where they discovered gravitational waves in February 2016. These places work continuously on the edge, the edge of possibility. They and others are reaching deeper and deeper into the unknowable every day, coming to know it and, at the same time, discovering more and more layers of profound and myste-rious stuff they don't yet know. All of this means that we ordinary non-science mortals have to change our philosophies too, change our ways of looking at things, and give up the concept of 'normal' for it just does not exist, except in our heads. As the old adage says, 'The more you know, the more you know you don't know.'

Merlin, the threshold keeper and guardian of doorways, teaches us to know this in our bones. Once we begin to live in that instant between past and future, instead of the sort of virtual world most of us inhabit, we find our lives change and grow and become more fulfilling. Merlin lurks at places and times where the opportunity for us to step out of our old life occurs, he waits there for us to choose to take that step across the threshold into strangeness ... the strangeness that is truly reality. I live at such a place, in that reality, on the edge between past and future, and this Wildman, Merlin, has been at my elbow all my life.

I've had a wild, crazy, sometimes mad-seeming life to outside watchers. For instance, I've been a dancer, barmaid, actress, car mechanic, artist and potter, horsewoman, civil servant, project manager, systems analyst and designer, Royal Horticultural Society award winning gardener, bushcraft woman, and currently writer and teacher ... just to mention a few! Things happen, they change and grow, offer me new opportunities and ten-to-one I go for it and take them. I'm willing to take risks, I don't have to know what's going to happen before I begin something, I adore being spontaneous. And all of that is so very useful when you're on the spirit-path. Having Merlin at my elbow all my life has helped enormously with all this. He's a really good friend, and that includes being a trickster par excellence who will tease and joke me into doing things I hadn't even dreamed of two minutes earlier. He tells me life, the universe and everything is composed of thresholds ... and, by damn, he's right!

I've been married to a mad scientist (with a strong spirit-bent too) for more than 40 years now so I get all the quantum and particle physics stuff over the breakfast table. Add to this that the man is actually able to talk about all this incredible stuff in terms of 'the cat sat on the mat' rather than needing blackboards full of equations to make his point. This is a serious advantage and has helped keep us together all this long time. When I ask about things like neutrons, or chaos, or nuclear fusion I get answers that I can understand – that's me, who has no maths or physics or chemistry even to 'O' level! In his youth he used to work at the Rutherford-Appleton Laboratories in Oxfordshire, which sounds seriously good fun from his stories. One of the stories he tells is about an experiment they did watching photons passing through a vacuum; at the end the professor in charge of the experiment said the only way he could explain the result was watching the ghost of a particle moving backwards in time! Ooooof! So this is the kind of science I've had with the cornflakes every morning for the past 40-odd years ... it tends to stretch the envelope. And yes, he knows Merlin too.

And science is another way Merlin uses to show us the world. It's easier for some than all this airy-fairy spiritual stuff! What

I've found, living with Paul all these years, is that once you stop putting things in boxes but allow them to relate across to each other then you begin to see how they are all different ways of saying similar things.

I had this from childhood too as my Dad was an engineer, and a racing driver back before WWII who raced alongside people like Stirling Moss's father. His family had lots of crossovers between the 'normal' and the 'not normal' as they were much involved with Helena Blavatsky, and my cousin Esther Bright was dear friends with Annie Bessant, indeed her mother, Great Aunt Ursula, bought the Benares Centre in India for the Theosophical Society. They also knew Rudolf Steiner. So the engineer-dad also knew the weirdos of his family. His first wife was a 'country-woman' of south Dartmoor who had grown up in the old ways, it's her brother who I always knew as Uncle Jack. Then he married my mother and her mother was a witch from the Isle of Mann, so I was steeped in all that stuff from birth and even before … Mum and Dad knew the exact moment they conceived me. And, of course, Dad knew Merlin too.

Merlin is a liminal master who is only too pleased to help facilitate all this knowing across borders. The borders come from us, from our minds and our own cultures; they're not real, not even in the sense our sun is real, or our planet, or the cosmos itself. The borders are constructions we make because contemplating all that hugeness can be very scary. Getting to know Merlin intimately, as a friend, helps you climb out of that box.

Merlin works towards integration … the bringing together of the many, many threads, indeed all the threads of the cosmos. He makes me think of the mycorrhiza, the fungi that connect all the trees and plants with each other – and so with all animals, and us too as without plants we cannot live, and with the mineral kingdom as without those too we can none of us live. He is a master of threads, the interconnecting energies that hold the universe together while at the same time allowing it to expand.

And all that takes me back to my mad-scientist husband again ... string theory and dark energy and dark matter. If you allow your brain to step over the normality-thresholds of the current text books, and the perceived wisdom, the connections between what we call science and the world of spirit make a lot of sense.

There are lots of thresholds throughout our lives, even waking up each morning is one! The bigger (perhaps?) and better realised ones include – birth, going to school, puberty, wedding, mothering, cronehood, mourning loss and bereavement, moving home, first going to work, changing your job, retirement, and death. We all do them. The more consciously we cross these thresholds the better.

Merlin as Guardian of Death

Death is the threshold that scares most people silly. Leaving this life that we've come to know for four-score-years-and-ten, or whatever the latest figure is, is so frightening for most people they try never to think of it. People run from the idea, won't talk about it, won't make their will. They shield their children from any possible encounter with it and generally screw up themselves and their offspring. And all this to run from the only absolute certainty in life ... that you will one day die. Death is a threshold, and so is birth, they're the same one but in opposite directions as Merlin has shown me.

We cross the threshold between otherworld and thisworld as we are conceived. At conception, our spirit leaves otherworld and begins to inhabit the growing spacesuit-body we and our parents have begun to create for us in our mother's womb. Nine months later we explode into the world through a lot of very hard work on our own and our mother's parts as we get born. It's an amazing process and one most of us forget almost immediately after going through it. Usually our spirit, and our friends in otherworld, don't wish our personal self to remember as this can inhibit us from doing what we decided to do this time around.

Too much knowledge can be a block! Some of us do remember, I'm one of those, but most don't. That is another thing Merlin helps us learn to reconnect with.

We celebrate the transition of birth, our entry into thisworld … but we *don't* celebrate our exit from thisworld with the same joy. We don't recognise and rejoice in a person's death and concomitant entry into otherworld in the same way. Usually, we commiserate death, we're sad, may say what a shame it is the person has died, especially if they're young. It hasn't always been like this, our ancestors celebrated death, and a lively wake is always good. Yes, there's the sadness that you won't be able to speak with, cuddle, enjoy the company of, make love with, that particular person any more but … but … we will know that spirit again. Our ancestors, and those of us who still follow the old ways, *know* reincarnation. It's not a vague belief, not a hope, it's an absolute knowing, we know it in our very bones. Once you know in this way you understand that you never lose contact with other spirits, they're always there even if they're no longer in bodies.

I experienced this very strongly at the age of three-and-a-half when my mother died of cancer. She'd been ill for about eighteen months, gradually getting worse. There was little the doctors could do in the early 1950s and, in any case, Mum had thought it was just tummy-ache and indigestion so had not gone to the doctor early. She stayed at home until the very last days so I was always able to see her, sit and play with her, talk with her, and I remember it well. And Merlin was there too, with her and with me. He would talk to me when I went to bed at night and when I was out in my special place at the bottom of the garden. I would see his shadowy figure in a corner of Mum's bedroom and so would Mum. Every now and then she'd glance up with a half-smile at the corner where he was sat. Dad said he was there at the end, with them in the hospital, when Mum finally passed across the threshold.

Dad took me to the funeral too, despite her sisters', my aunts, horror at the thought of it! They weren't connected like Mum was, she was a seventh child of a seventh child, which makes the connections very strong. I'm so glad Dad took me to see her off. In my own little child's way, I knew what was going on – children do you know, despite what grownups think. I knew I'd not see Mum again in this life, but I also knew she was not gone forever, that she was still there in spirit, for spirit was all around me then and completely part of my life. As we stood by the graveside I asked Dad, 'Mummy's not in the box, is she?' He looked up at the sun and replied, 'No. She's gone home, she's better, no more pain. And we'll see her again.' So there were none of the abandonment-traumas children suffer when they don't really know the person is gone. I've never forgotten and it made life so much more possible without her. Many years later, at the wake after my Dad's funeral, my 25-year-old nephew asked, 'Grandad wasn't in the box, was he?' ... I was so pleased to be able to answer him in the same way Dad had answered me 40-odd years before.

Sleep and Dreams

Merlin is guardian of all thresholds, including the one we cross at birth and death. He will help us learn to cross over, in both directions, and he does this by teaching us what happens when we sleep. Like Prospero says in Shakespeare's Tempest, *'We are such stuff as dreams are made on; and our little life is rounded with a sleep.'* and so it is. The transit between waking and sleeping is yet another threshold and each of us crosses it every day. As Merlin told me, it's practice for how to do dying so my work with him has always (right from those baby-dreams in my cot) included daily dream-work.

In the early days it was good that he would be there, helping me cross over each night as I went to sleep, and helping me cross back again in the morning. Like all journeying, at first the going is often easier than the coming back, or at least coming back with true memory of what happened, of where you've been and what you've done and learned.

Dad helped by telling me one of our fairy stories. It's about a young man who crosses the borders into the realm of the Faer and meets with the fairy queen. She takes him into her realm, cossets him and eventually sets him on the road home with a bag of gold, telling him to take care how he crosses back. He goes galumphing gaily off, crosses the border and arrives back home, very full of himself. He opens the bag triumphantly before his relatives only to find it's full of stones, not gold at all. He's completely crestfallen and all his relations laugh at him so he sneaks off and manages (after various trials and tribulations) to get back into fairyland. At first the queen will have none of him, but he is now humble and willing to listen and learn. He learns how to go back across the border consciously and sets off again full of care, deliberately and knowingly, with the bag of gold the queen has given him. This time he makes it, crosses and the bag is still full of gold, not the stones of his carelessness.

Merlin helped me take this to heart and learn it so I'm able to cross, there-and-back-again as Bilbo puts it, between the worlds of dream and the everyday, and bring back the wisdom-gold all intact. All any of us have to do is ask him to help and he will, as long as we mean it and are committed to learning.

Esplumoir: Merlin's Translation

Vivien is strongly associated with Merlin's translation although it's usually misinterpreted as her putting him away after stealing his magic. What she really does is to help him into and through his translation, transformation and transmutation.

In the stories his translation takes many forms – within a hawthorn tree, within the stone by the fountain of Barenton, in the crystal cave, in the crystal tower, but perhaps the most intriguing of them all is in the esplumoir.

The origin of the word esplumoir is shrouded in almost as

much mystery as Merlin himself, which is not, perhaps, surprising. People suggest it comes from a word related to falconry, which indeed it may, saying an esplumoir is a dark, warm place where a hawk or falcon is put at the time of the moult. A falconer-friend says this just ain't the case, you don't put the birds in dark boxes, but it's a good story and gives an idea of Merlin's process.

Most importantly, it's said that this is where the bird *sings up his own feathers*.

That always stuns me. And it makes sense within my bones too. To sing up your own feathers sounds a wonderful thing to do. It makes me think of the wonderful dawn chorus the birds give us during the late spring when they call their territories and sing out for a mate. It also calls up the whole concept of enchantment. To enchant something, as you'll remember, is to sing it to life. In his esplumoir, Merlin sings himself back into life, renews himself and makes himself ready for the new time (the now-time) that he comes to help.

So Merlin goes into his esplumoir; the moulting cage; the falcon's mew; the place where the old cloak of feathers is shed and the new one is grown; the place of transformation and where he renews his shape, his form, his matter, the place of transmutation where he reinvents his essence.

Short Aside on Transmutation ...

- To transform something is to change its form, its shape
- To transmute something is to change its essence

Let's play the science game ... first of all, there are *stable* elements (metals), which means those that don't emit particles; such metals include lead and gold. And then there are *unstable* elements/metals, those that do emit particles like uranium. We call them radioactive.

The unstable elements all change. It's part of their nature, what they do. They transmute themselves from unstable to stable and they do this by losing mass (weight) ... they go to weight-watchers you might say! They lose mass/weight by emitting particles, losing particles, giving off neutrons and protons, shedding mass, getting lighter. Uranium wobbles along, dropping neutrons and protons, and picking up the occasional proton, until it goes from being an unstable metal, uranium, to becoming a stable one, lead.

Uranium hasn't changed its *form*, it hasn't put on a new suit of clothes. It has changed the fundamental particles of which it is made, it's changed its essence.

This is transmutation.

Let's follow another interesting thought ... the supreme quest of alchemy is to transmute lead into gold.

Lead has the atomic number 82 and gold the atomic number 79. These atomic numbers are defined by the number of protons each element possesses so changing the element, transmutation, requires changing the number of protons (positive particles). You can't do this by any chemical means.

Because lead is a stable element, i.e. it's not emitting particles, to *force* it to release three protons – the number difference between 82 and 79 – and so transmute into gold (another stable, non-emitting element), requires a vast input of energy. You need a huge nuclear reactor (or a handy passing supernova!) to make it happen. In nature, the element gold was likely made inside a supernova some 4.5+ billion years ago, before the formation of planet Earth.

But, and here's the fun bit, the transmutation of lead into gold isn't just theoretically possible, it was actually achieved in 1980 when Glenn Seaborg, the 1951 Nobel Laureate in Chemistry, succeeded in transmuting a minute quantity of lead into gold. There's also an earlier report, from 1972, by Soviet physicists at a nuclear research facility near Lake Baikal in Siberia. They accidentally discovered that a reaction had turned lead into gold when they found the lead shielding of an experimental reactor had changed to gold. There's no more available on this, unfortunately.

Back to the Esplumoir ...

Short aside over!

So when Merlin goes into his esplumoir to transmute himself it might be good to think of all the above. He isn't changing his clothes, his form, he's changing the very substance of which he is made. He changes his essence, changes the energy particles of which he is made, and this requires, even in spirit-terms, an incredible energy-force to effect.

It's worth remembering that energy is not itself an object, not a thing, not matter! An atom is an object, a thing; energy is not. So Merlin's translation is not a change of form, of matter, it's a change of energy. His time in the esplumoir is about transmuting himself to a new level of energy, one that's suitable for his next job on Planet Earth. Perhaps, one day, he will transmute himself into gold, or its equivalent for wizards.

The esplumoir can also be likened to the athenor in alchemy, the oven that burns off the dross – the stuff that's past its sell-by date – and reveals the good new stuff inside.

The story of transmutation, this process that occurs through incredible heat like that inside a supernova, reminds me of the story of the phoenix. The phoenix spontaneously combusts and is reduced to ashes, it then remakes itself out of the ashes to become again the firebird, the sun-bird, the Chanticleer who crows the coming of the sun. And many images for the sun are of a winged disc, like a bird. I sense this is what Merlin does.

This connection with the sun again draws me back to the incredible transmutation process. A supernova is an exploding/exploded sun and our own sun will do this one day towards the end of its incarnation. I find this stunning. In its death-throws, the sun will again create all the atoms and elements – and the energy – for life, new life somewhere else. We're back to cycles and breathing again. No big bang but a continuous breathing in and breathing out cycle that spirals into new layers, strata. It feels like what Ursula le Guin speaks of in *The Left Hand of Darkness* when the hero speaks of the *augmentation of the complexity and intensity of the field of intelligent life*. For this is what life, the universe and everything wants, more complexity and intensity, and this is what Merlin wants us to help him to achieve.

Merlin, in the esplumoir, dies to his old self, to the wizard he has been, and that death (perhaps like the sun going supernova) enables the birth of the wizard he is to become.

9

Having a Relationship with Merlin

Relationship

Having a relationship with otherworldly beings has always involved some up-close-and-personal stuff and Merlin is no different. His own 'birth' is told in this same way, his mother is made love to by an otherworldly being. He offers this to all of us if we want it.

The Christian perspective, and that of most modern psychology, would like to call this sort of relationship possession, or a form of hearing voices, or schizophrenia. Schizophrenia is a long-term mental health condition that causes a range of different psychological symptoms, including hallucinations and what is called hearing or seeing things that do not exist. Doctors often describe schizophrenia as a psychotic illness, meaning severely mentally ill, insane, mad, certifiable. The fear of being labelled anything like that is a good reason for keeping your head down and not talking about any experiences that people might think show you're unhinged. But that fear doesn't stop the strange things happening, nor the odd-seeming relationships with otherworldly beings.

I've been a part the psychology world since 1990, as a transpersonal psychotherapist, and in my London practice I had several clients who had had these sorts of experience. I was fortunate in my training to be with two of the founders of transpersonal psychology in Britain, Ian Gordon-Brown and Barbara Somers, neither of whom had any problems with otherworldly experiences. In consequence, I was able to pass on their wisdom to the poor clients whose worst fear was that they would be sectioned! It's unnerving still to see how many people stuff their experiences because they know of no-one to talk with about them, and fear of ridicule or maybe much worse keeps them silent. I wish this would change.

The transpersonal is a big part of the collection of goodies I've acquired in my 60-plus years of *cauldroning* – meaning collecting wisdom into one's own cauldron, the shell that holds our spirit in incarnation. Merlin encouraged me to go get the training by first making sure I'd go to a talk, which I otherwise never would have, to hear this incredible man whose name I hadn't registered at all when he began speaking. When he finished I rushed up to him saying, 'Where do I sign on?' Ian Gordon-Brown (the speaker) looked at me with a twinkle in his eye, I was by no means the first person to do this after one of his talks, and gave me the phone number and address. I was on my introductory transpersonal workshop within a month. I learned, long after the training when Ian was my mentor while I was in practice, that he too knew Merlin, very differently from me but just as intimately.

For the final anecdote of my relationship with Merlin I thought I'd give you my first seriously intimate, up-close-and-personal experience with him which happened while I was at university.

Dancing the Light

I was one of the first people to take a degree in Modern Educational Dance, indeed it was my tutor who began the degree after long chats with us, his students. It was a very exciting time in my life and I was in the studio every day, working, dancing, choreographing and just plain practising for as many hours as I could manage. We were tasked with a project on using light as an active medium in the dance and I was fascinated by Newton's prism and its effects. I cornered one of the science tutors, one I'd only just noticed around, and asked him to help me. I wanted to dance the prism.

'Not hard,' said the science tutor, 'not hard at all,' sounding just like the druid in the Cauldrons of Poesy. He showed me how to position three spotlights – having first covered each light with a gel of red or blue or green – so that each of them fired onto exactly the same spot on the background wall. Then he said, 'Go on, get in that spot and dance!' So I did. Wow! I was covered in all the colours of the rainbow and, at the same time, my movements made shadows on the floor and walls that were also all the colours of the rainbow. He filmed the dance and that was my project, it got me full marks.

Now I must tell you this was all going on in the late 1960s, everyone was a hippie, students and most of the younger tutors too and this science man was no exception, nor was I. This man was in his late 20s, slim to wiry, good looking, not a bad dancer himself, and he looked fantastic in flares and the T-shirts of the time. Of course, the obvious happened and on the evening after the project was assessed, and I got full marks, we became lovers for just one night. We had hardly touched for the weeks until the project was finished. That wonderful sexual tension, where we both knew what we wanted … but not quite yet, really helped my dancing and so the film. The science tutor understood how important that was long before I did, putting me off gently when I would have seduced him.

Our first and only night together (for that time) was utterly incredible from my perspective. I'd never experienced love-making like it and it nearly blew my tiny mind to use an expression of the day. I woke in the pre-dawn and spent a while, leaning on one elbow, just looking at him sleeping, then I got up and went to stand by the window. The late crescent moon hung in the early sky with Venus at her tail. I stood there for ages, watching, until she was gradually obliterated by the growing dawn then I pulled my clothes on and left. I went down to sit by the estuary and watch the light on the sea and the waking birds beginning to feed – the Exe estuary is a famous bird and nature reserve. After a while, as I sat there, I felt a presence beside me.

'You enjoyed that, didn't you?' said the voice. I knew that

voice, had known it all my life.

'You?' I asked him. 'Yes, me,' was the reply. It dawned. 'It was you all the time? You being the science tutor?' He chuckled, 'Of course. I wouldn't leave you to do that work all by yourself now would I? You wanted to *experience* light, didn't you? Not just talk about it, make a picture of it, but *be* it, that's what you wanted isn't it?'

I nodded, and yes, that's what we'd done. Even the filming was about light, photons firing at the film and creating a pattern on it. I began to grin. 'Have you taken on a new profession then, as science tutor?' I asked him.

'Certainly not! Had you ever met me there before this project came up?' I hadn't of course. 'And you won't see me there again either,' he went on, which was only to be expected. 'But I may visit you again of a night, perhaps, if you'd like?'

And now a shadowy shifting human form seemed to be sitting on the sand beside me, it looked like the dark, wiry man in flares who had sparked the fires in me last night.

'I'd like ...' I said.

Merlin does that with all of us, all the people that I know who work with him, so it's not a lot of use being the jealous type! But then nothing in spirit, or in matter either, is ever 'yours', you own nothing but you may enjoy everything if you choose. Including Merlin.

Bibliography

These are just some of the books I've found fascinating to read about Merlin:

Jean Markale: *Merlin: Priest of Nature*

T. H. White: *The Once and Future King*

John Matthews: *Merlin: Shaman, Prophet, Magician* and *Merlin Through the Ages: A Chronological Anthology and Source Book*

R. J. Stewart: *Merlin: The Prophetic Vision and the Mystic Life*, *The Way of Merlin* and ed. *Walker Between Worlds* by Robert Kirk

James Dyer: *The Penguin Guide to Prehistoric England and Wales* (Penguin 1981)

Geoffrey of Monmouth: *The History of the Kings of Britain*, trans. Lewis Thorpe, (Penguin, St Ives 1966) and *Life of Merlin*, Vita Merlini, ed. and trans. B. Clarke, (Cardiff 1973)

Nennius: *British History and the Welsh Annals*, Latin and trans. John Morris, History from the Sources VIII, (Chichester 1980)

William Worcestre: *Itineraries*, edited from the unique MS. Corpus Christi College Cambridge, 210, Latin and trans. John Harvey, (Oxford 1969)

Sir Thomas Malory and Lord Alfred Tennyson: *Sir Gawain and the Green Knight, Le Morte d'Arthur* and *Idylls of the King*

Thomas Malory and Sir James Knowles: *The Legends of King Arthur and his Knights* (Empire Library)

Courtney Davis and Peter Quiller: *Merlin the Immortal*

Moon Books

PAGANISM & SHAMANISM

What is Paganism? A religion, a spirituality, an alternative belief system, nature worship? You can find support for all these definitions (and many more) in dictionaries, encyclopaedias, and text books of religion, but subscribe to any one and the truth will evade you. Above all Paganism is a creative pursuit, an encounter with reality, an exploration of meaning and an expression of the soul. Druids, Heathens, Wiccans and others, all contribute their insights and literary riches to the Pagan tradition. Moon Books invites you to begin or to deepen your own encounter, right here, right now. If you have enjoyed this book, why not tell other readers by posting a review on your preferred book site. Recent bestsellers from Moon Books are:

Journey to the Dark Goddess
How to Return to Your Soul
Jane Meredith
Discover the powerful secrets of the Dark Goddess and transform your depression, grief and pain into healing and integration.
Paperback: 978-1-84694-677-6 ebook: 978-1-78099-223-5

Shamanic Reiki
Expanded Ways of Working with Universal Life Force Energy
Llyn Roberts, Robert Levy
Shamanism and Reiki are each powerful ways of healing;
together, their power multiplies. *Shamanic Reiki* introduces
techniques to help healers and Reiki practitioners tap ancient
healing wisdom.
Paperback: 978-1-84694-037-8 ebook: 978-1-84694-650-9

Pagan Portals – The Awen Alone
Walking the Path of the Solitary Druid
Joanna van der Hoeven
An introductory guide for the solitary Druid, *The Awen Alone*
will accompany you as you explore, and seek out your own
place within the natural world.
Paperback: 978-1-78279-547-6 ebook: 978-1-78279-546-9

A Kitchen Witch's World of Magical Herbs & Plants
Rachel Patterson
A journey into the magical world of herbs and plants, filled with
magical uses, folklore, history and practical magic. By popular
writer, blogger and kitchen witch, Tansy Firedragon.
Paperback: 978-1-78279-621-3 ebook: 978-1-78279-620-6

Medicine for the Soul
The Complete Book of Shamanic Healing
Ross Heaven
All you will ever need to know about shamanic healing and
how to become your own shaman...
Paperback: 978-1-78099-419-2 ebook: 978-1-78099-420-8

Shaman Pathways – The Druid Shaman
Exploring the Celtic Otherworld
Danu Forest

A practical guide to Celtic shamanism with exercises and techniques as well as traditional lore for exploring the Celtic Otherworld.
Paperback: 978-1-78099-615-8 ebook: 978-1-78099-616-5

Traditional Witchcraft for the Woods and Forests
A Witch's Guide to the Woodland with Guided Meditations and Pathworking
Melusine Draco
A Witch's guide to walking alone in the woods, with guided meditations and pathworking.
Paperback: 978-1-84694-803-9 ebook: 978-1-84694-804-6

Wild Earth, Wild Soul
A Manual for an Ecstatic Culture
Bill Pfeiffer
Imagine a nature-based culture so alive and so connected, spreading like wildfire. This book is the first flame...
Paperback: 978-1-78099-187-0 ebook: 978-1-78099-188-7

Naming the Goddess
Trevor Greenfield
Naming the Goddess is written by over eighty adherents and scholars of Goddess and Goddess Spirituality.
Paperback: 978-1-78279-476-9 ebook: 978-1-78279-475-2

Shapeshifting into Higher Consciousness
Heal and Transform Yourself and Our World with Ancient Shamanic and Modern Methods
Llyn Roberts
Ancient and modern methods that you can use every day to transform yourself and make a positive difference in the world.
Paperback: 978-1-84694-843-5 ebook: 978-1-84694-844-2

Readers of ebooks can buy or view any of these bestsellers by clicking on the live link in the title. Most titles are published in paperback and as an ebook. Paperbacks are available in traditional bookshops. Both print and ebook formats are available online.

Find more titles and sign up to our readers' newsletter at http://www.johnhuntpublishing.com/paganism. Follow us on Facebook at https://www.facebook.com/MoonBooks and Twitter at https://twitter.com/MoonBooksJHP.